Queen Victoria's Grandchildren

Queen Victoria's Grandchildren

Lance Salway

COLLINS & BROWN

First published in Great Britain in 1991
by Collins & Brown Limited
Mercury House
195 Knightsbridge
London SW7 1RE

A CIP catalogue record for this book
is available from the British Library

ISBN 1 85585 078 8

Conceived, edited, designed and produced by
Signpost Books, Ltd
25 Eden Drive, Headington, Oxford OX3 0AB

Editor: Dorothy Wood
Designer: Gillian Riley
Paste up: Naomi Games
Decorations: Saint Bride Printing Library

Typeset by Goodfellow & Egan, Cambridge
Reproduction by Fotographics, Ltd
Printed and bound in Hong Kong by Everbest, Ltd

Introduction

Queen Victoria was forty years old when her first grandchild, the future Kaiser Wilhelm II, was born in 1859. By the time that her last, Prince Maurice of Battenberg, was born over thirty years later, the Queen was seventy-two, and grandmother to forty princes and princesses scattered across Europe from Russia to Romania and from Sweden to Spain.

Queen Victoria enjoyed her grandchildren in small doses. Although she liked children, she could not tolerate 'their being idolised and made too great objects of – or having a number of them about me making a great noise.' And even though she herself was the mother of nine children – only one of whom, Princess Louise, was childless, she disapproved of large families, regarding them as 'a misfortune'.

As the years passed, the Queen found it increasingly difficult to be a satisfactory grandmother to such a rapidly multiplying throng. Yet, despite her aversion to childbirth and babies, the Queen took a keen interest in every royal pregnancy and insisted on being present at the births of her grandchildren whenever possible. She would then keep a stern but affectionate eye on their conduct and education as they grew up and later immerse herself in the ever interesting task of finding them a suitable husband or wife.

As well as her characteristic qualities of honesty, common sense and a strong sense of duty, Queen Victoria was to pass a darker legacy to her grandchildren. There was no history of haemophilia in the families of the Queen or the Prince Consort, but Queen Victoria transmitted it to her own son, Leopold, and to her daughters, Alice and Beatrice.

For all her benign concern for the personal and domestic happiness of her forty grandchildren, Queen Victoria was powerless to prevent this affliction, which was to have so tragic an effect on their lives.

Contents

Introduction
Family Tree

Queen Victoria's Grandchildren

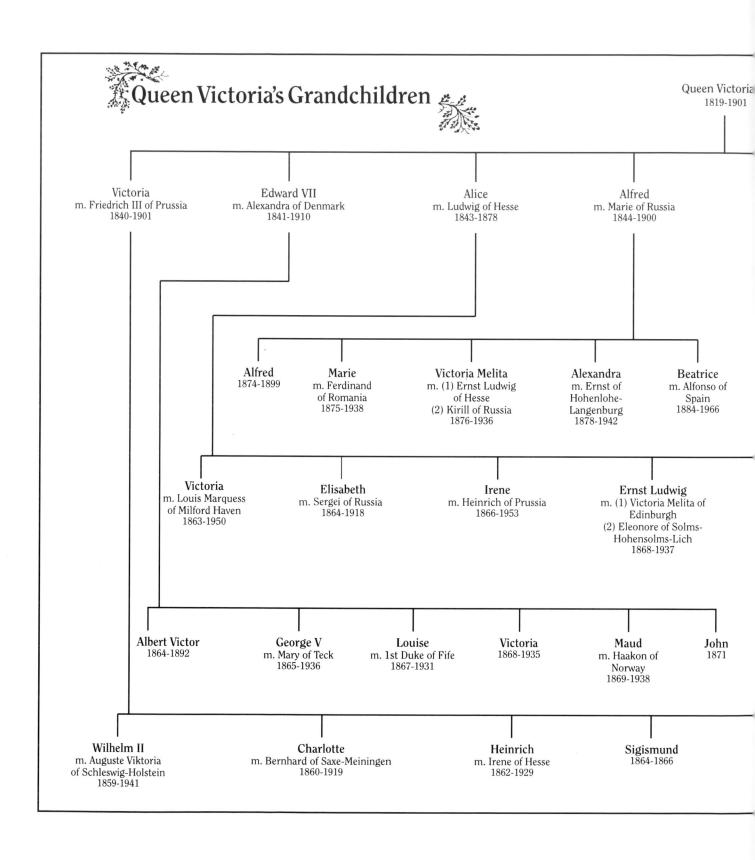

Queen Victoria
1819-1901

Victoria
m. Friedrich III of Prussia
1840-1901

Edward VII
m. Alexandra of Denmark
1841-1910

Alice
m. Ludwig of Hesse
1843-1878

Alfred
m. Marie of Russia
1844-1900

Alfred
1874-1899

Marie
m. Ferdinand
of Romania
1875-1938

Victoria Melita
m. (1) Ernst Ludwig
of Hesse
(2) Kirill of Russia
1876-1936

Alexandra
m. Ernst of
Hohenlohe-
Langenburg
1878-1942

Beatrice
m. Alfonso of
Spain
1884-1966

Victoria
m. Louis Marquess
of Milford Haven
1863-1950

Elisabeth
m. Sergei of Russia
1864-1918

Irene
m. Heinrich of Prussia
1866-1953

Ernst Ludwig
m. (1) Victoria Melita of
Edinburgh
(2) Eleonore of Solms-
Hohensolms-Lich
1868-1937

Albert Victor
1864-1892

George V
m. Mary of Teck
1865-1936

Louise
m. 1st Duke of Fife
1867-1931

Victoria
1868-1935

Maud
m. Haakon of
Norway
1869-1938

John
1871

Wilhelm II
m. Auguste Viktoria
of Schleswig-Holstein
1859-1941

Charlotte
m. Bernhard of Saxe-Meiningen
1860-1919

Heinrich
m. Irene of Hesse
1862-1929

Sigismund
1864-1866

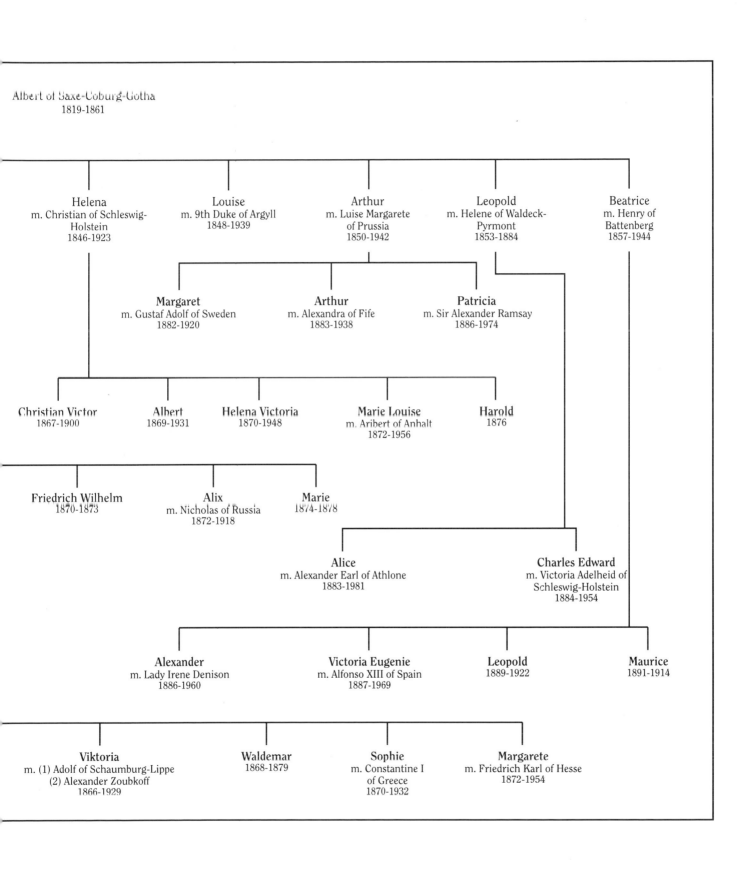

Albert of Saxe-Coburg-Gotha
1819-1861

Helena
m. Christian of Schleswig-
Holstein
1846-1923

Louise
m. 9th Duke of Argyll
1848-1939

Arthur
m. Luise Margarete
of Prussia
1850-1942

Leopold
m. Helene of Waldeck-
Pyrmont
1853-1884

Beatrice
m. Henry of
Battenberg
1857-1944

Margaret
m. Gustaf Adolf of Sweden
1882-1920

Arthur
m. Alexandra of Fife
1883-1938

Patricia
m. Sir Alexander Ramsay
1886-1974

Christian Victor
1867-1900

Albert
1869-1931

Helena Victoria
1870-1948

Marie Louise
m. Aribert of Anhalt
1872-1956

Harold
1876

Friedrich Wilhelm
1870-1873

Alix
m. Nicholas of Russia
1872-1918

Marie
1874-1878

Alice
m. Alexander Earl of Athlone
1883-1981

Charles Edward
m. Victoria Adelheid of
Schleswig-Holstein
1884-1954

Alexander
m. Lady Irene Denison
1886-1960

Victoria Eugenie
m. Alfonso XIII of Spain
1887-1969

Leopold
1889-1922

Maurice
1891-1914

Viktoria
m. (1) Adolf of Schaumburg-Lippe
(2) Alexander Zoubkoff
1866-1929

Waldemar
1868-1879

Sophie
m. Constantine I
of Greece
1870-1932

Margarete
m. Friedrich Karl of Hesse
1872-1954

The Children of Victoria and Friedrich

Wilhelm II
German Emperor
1859–1941

Charlotte
Duchess of Saxe-Meiningen
1860–1919

Heinrich
Prince of Prussia
1862–1929

Sigismund
Prince of Prussia
1864–1866

Viktoria
Princess Adolf of Schaumburg-Lippe
1866–1929

Waldemar
Prince of Prussia
1868–1879

Sophie
Queen of Greece
1870–1932

Margarete
Landgravine of Hesse
1872–1954

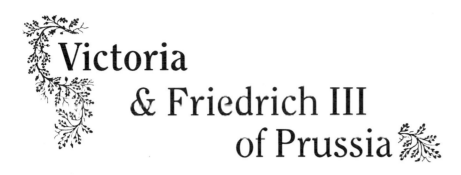

Victoria & Friedrich III of Prussia

Queen Victoria and Prince Albert had hoped that their first child would be a boy, but the Queen's initial disappointment soon turned to affection, though she took care to distance herself from the physical care of the infant princess. She did not dislike babies, but she found them ugly and 'frog-like', and had no inclination to nurse any of her children. Albert was a more devoted and anxious parent than his wife, and he adored his daughter from the first.

The princess was christened Victoria Adelaide Mary Louise, but she was known as Pussy until she was seven and as Vicky after that. She soon proved to be a child of exceptional intelligence, willing and eager to learn, and her father found her an ideal pupil. Prince Albert had long cherished the dream of seeing the small states of Germany united into one democratic country under the leadership of Prussia, and he saw a marriage between Vicky and the heir to the Prussian throne as a means of passing his progressive, liberal ideas to future generations of the Prussian monarchy.

Prince Friedrich Wilhelm of Prussia, known as Fritz, was therefore invited to Dalmoral, and he and Vicky fell in love. She was then only fourteen and their marriage would have to wait three years, but an alliance between Britain and Prussia was now in prospect.

But Albert's plans came to nothing. Emperor Wilhelm I resented his son's ideas and was influenced solely by the Chancellor, Otto von Bismarck. Fritz had to wait over thirty years before he ascended the throne, in 1888, but he was by then ill with cancer of the throat, and he reigned for only ninety-eight days.

Vicky spent the rest of her life alone and embittered, at odds with her capricious son, Wilhelm II. Only in the company of her youngest daughters and their families did she achieve any happiness in the bleak years of her widowhood. In 1901, she too died of cancer, having outlived her mother by less than a year.

Fritz and Vicky, Crown Prince and Princess of Prussia in 1865 with their children (left to right) *Prince Wilhelm, Prince Sigismund* (baby) *Prince Heinrich and Princess Charlotte.*

Queen Victoria's first grandchild was born in Berlin on 27 January, 1859, and she wasted no time in sending congratulations to her daughter. 'God be praised for all his mercies, and for bringing you safely through this awful time!' she wrote. 'Our joy, our gratitude know no bounds.'

The birth had been difficult and dangerous, and for a time it was feared that both mother and child might die. As it was, the child's left arm was dislocated during the birth, but by the time this was noticed by the English midwife, Mrs Innocent, it was too late to rectify the damage. The arm and the hand remained stunted and useless, a disability that was to have a profound effect on the character of the young Prince.

Wilhelm's upbringing was austere and disciplined but his progress disappointed Vicky and Fritz. The child was lively and intelligent but he proved backward at learning to read and write and showed no aptitude for study. His withered arm seemed a continual reproach to Vicky, and she made no allowance for his disability. He was forced to ride, shoot and play games as though he had no handicap whatsoever and, at the same time, he was compelled to endure a succession of appalling treatments intended to correct and cure the defect. None of the treatments worked and Wilhelm's arm remained useless for the rest of his life. He overcame his handicap with considerable courage, and he became a competent pianist and tennis player.

Wilhelm soon came under the influence of his tyrannical German grandmother, the Empress Augusta, who spoiled him, bribed him and stimulated the development of that 'terrible Prussian pride' that his parents had hoped to discourage. The Emperor and Empress disliked and mistrusted Vicky, fearing the influence of England on her husband and son, and they set about alienating Wilhelm from his parents, happily assisted in the enterprise by the Chancellor, Otto von Bismarck. He was determined to exercise complete control over the

Wilhelm as a small child. His mother blamed herself for his withered arm, regarding it as shameful and loathsome.

Wilhelm with his grandmother, Queen Victoria (left). *Even as a small boy he enjoyed dressing up* (centre), *a fascination which he carried to extreme lengths when he was older* (right).

future Kaiser, and by lies and flattery he succeeded in convincing Wilhelm of his own invincible superiority and of the duplicity of his English mother.

Wilhelm spent the ninety-eight days of his father's reign preparing for his own succession. Fritz was mortally ill with cancer of the throat, and it was only a matter of time before his son became Emperor in his place. When Fritz died, Wilhelm immediately sealed off the Neues Paleis in Potsdam. He was convinced that his mother had been passing state secrets to Britain. No evidence was found, of course, but this did not dispel Wilhelm's pathological suspicions of his mother, or his own feelings of insecurity.

Wilhelm was now in a position of enormous power, the ruler of Europe's richest industrial nation with prosperous overseas colonies, and the capability of attaining military superiority over Britain and France. But he was poorly equipped to assume this responsibility. He was lazy, impatient and too restless to concentrate on the detailed work of government. His ministers found him impossible to deal with: he was convinced that he knew best, that his opinion was infallible and his conduct beyond reproach. He hated long letters and documents, often throwing them away unread or else annotating them with facile comments.

Much more to Wilhelm's taste were the ostentatious displays of imperial grandeur that characterised his reign. He was besotted with the emblems of militaristic display – elaborate uniforms, gleaming swords, plumed helmets, military music. He travelled in a solid gold helmet and possessed an astonishing variety of uniforms, many of which he had designed himself. Even as a child he was obsessed by uniforms; when he was eight years old he had asked Queen Victoria for 'an English uniform' as a birthday present, and when he was ten he was commissioned by his grandfather as a lieutenant in the 2nd Pomeranian Regiment.

These trappings of military display helped Wilhelm to conceal his feelings of insecurity, but his life and reign were filled with such contradictions. He was shy, sensitive and intelligent, yet he did all he could to appear cruel and ruthless. And his moods were unpredictable. One moment he could be sadistic, turning his rings inwards so that the stones cut into the palms of people with whom he shook hands, and the next he could be charming and considerate. He was devoted to his wife, the plump and placid Auguste Viktoria of Schleswig-Holstein-Sonderburg-Augustenburg, and their seven children, but he did not hesitate to regulate the lives of other close relations.

The First World War was an inevitable consequence of the growth of the German military machine and Wilhelm's hatred of Britain – his war games now became painfully real, costing the German nation two million lives and five million more crippled and wounded. At the war's end the disillusion and despair of the German people brought the House of Hohenzollern to its knees. Had Wilhelm abdicated, as he was advised, then the Hohenzollerns might have remained on their throne but, as always, Wilhelm thought he knew best. In the end he was forced into exile in Holland, where he spent the last twenty years of his life leading the quiet life of a country gentleman – growing roses, drinking English tea, and reading the novels of P.G. Wodehouse.

Wilhelm's declining years may have been tranquil but the same could not be said for the lives of his children. His eldest son, the playboy Crown Prince Wilhelm – known to the British as 'Little Willy' – took refuge from his stormy marriage to Princess Cecilie of Mecklenburg-Schwerin in the arms of a succession of mistresses. His brother, Prince Eitel Friedrich, was equally ardent in his pursuit of young men, and his marriage of convenience to a plain Duchess of Oldenburg was, not surprisingly childless and ended in divorce: Unlike his elder

From an early age Wilhelm II was obsessed by uniforms and other emblems of militaristic display.

brothers, Prince Adalbert was happily married and led a quiet life out of the public eye. Prince August Wilhelm became a fervent Nazi, and Prince Oskar married one of his mother's ladies-in-waiting. Wilhelm's youngest son, Prince Joachim, was unhappily married and subject to fits of depression. He committed suicide in 1920. Wilhelm's only daughter, Viktoria Luise, married Prince Ernst August of Hanover; their children included the future Queen Frederica of Greece.

The Empress Auguste Viktoria never recovered from the shock of Joachim's death, and the fact that she and Wilhelm were forbidden to attend the funeral in Germany only exacerbated her grief. She died a few months later. The following year Wilhelm married the widowed Princess Hermine von Schönaich-Carolath, who was thirty years his junior.

Wilhelm II, third and last Emperor of Germany, died in 1941. Once the most bellicose of monarchs, he had behaved with remarkable dignity and discretion during his later years. He left instructions that his body should not be returned for a state funeral in Germany, but instead be buried at his home in Holland, the country that had sheltered him with such kindness in the long years of his exile.

Wilhelm in uncharacteristically sober garb, with his first wife, the Empress Auguste Viktoria (above). After her death, he married the widowed Princess Hermine von Schönaich-Carolath (right), who was thirty years his junior and the mother of five children.

Charlotte, Duchess of Saxe-Meiningen
1860–1919

The birth of the Princess Royal's second child on 24 July, 1860, was far less traumatic than the first had been. The labour was easy, the birth trouble free, and the infant proved to be a daughter.

The child was christened Viktoria Elisabeth Auguste Charlotte but Queen Victoria's hopes that the infant princess might be called by her own name were dashed when Vicky informed her that the child was to be known as Charlotte.

Vicky's elder daughter proved to be just as difficult and troublesome as her brother, Wilhelm. Charlotte was much influenced by her elder brother and, like him, she proved to be slow and reluctant to learn. Her behaviour also left a lot to be desired. 'She is a most difficult child to bring up,' Vicky complained to her mother. 'If she were not so stupid and backward her being naughty would not matter.' Vicky continued to complain to her mother about Charlotte's lack of interest in reading and art, and about her appearance. 'She has grown very stout,' she noted when Charlotte was seventeen. 'She is most ungraceful when she moves and walks, sticks out her elbows and trundles about . . . She also has her Papa's hands and feet which for a young girl is most unfortunate.'

For her part, Charlotte criticised everything her parents said and did. Like Wilhelm, she was spoiled by the Empress Augusta, who may not have encouraged Charlotte's antagonism towards her parents but nonetheless did nothing to prevent it.

In 1877, Charlotte fell in love with Prince Bernhard of Saxe-Meiningen, a university friend of her elder brother, and they were married the following year. In May 1879 their only daughter, Feodora, was born, making Queen Victoria a great-grandmother at the age of fifty-nine. The arrival of her own first grandchild gave Vicky little pleasure, for it came only fifteen days after the death from diphtheria of her youngest son, Waldemar.

Despite her marriage, Charlotte remained bored and discontented,

Princess Charlotte at the age of thirteen.

Even as an adult Charlotte continued to make mischief among her relations. One of her cousins remembered her as 'one of the most changeable women I have ever had to do with'.

resenting all criticism and continuing to scheme with Wilhelm and Bernhard against her parents. She spent much of her time visiting relations in the various royal courts of Europe, and she was a frequent visitor to Coburg, where her uncle, Prince Alfred, was now the reigning Duke. Alfred's eldest daughter, Marie, was enchanted by her sophsticated Cousin Charly. 'Never have I heard a softer, more melodious voice,' Maria remembered later. 'There was a purr in it which would have disarmed an ogre.' The young Coburg princesses were fascinated by the delicate aroma of the cigarettes that Charlotte smoked ceaselessly, by her apparent knowledge of horses and flowers, by her fascination with politics. 'She could be more charming than anyone I have ever known,' Marie recalled. 'She was, for all that, one of the most changeable women I have ever had to do with.'

Charlotte was to play a vital part in Marie's life for it was she who suggested and arranged her young cousin's marriage to Prince Ferdinand of Romania. She acted as an intermediary between Marie's family and the Hohenzollerns, and it was she who eventually persuaded the timid, embarrassed Prince to propose.

It was when Marie was at last married and installed in Bucharest, as Crown Princess of Romania, that she began to see the darker side of her fascinating cousin. 'Having been the chief promoter of our marriage, she felt that she had the right to profit by the results.' Charlotte made annual visits to Romania, ostensibly to visit Marie, but in reality to ingratiate herself with her father-in-law, the forbidding King Carol. Charlotte pulled Marie to pieces behind her back, spread scandalous gossip about her behaviour, and stimulated ill-feeling between Kaiser Wilhelm and the King. Despite this duplicity, Marie found it difficult to abandon her affection for Charlotte. 'Even after I had discovered what a false friend she was, her soft, purring voice could awaken again that old sensation of delight she had given me when I was a child.'

Vicky, of course, was well aware of Charlotte's devious nature. 'She and Bernhard take the *reverse* view of what *I* do on almost every *subject*, and abuse me right and left behind my back,' she wrote to her daughter Sophie, by now Crown Princess of Greece. 'She makes so much mischief and gets herself and others into too many scrapes.'

As time passed, Charlotte's attitude towards her mother mellowed, but she was never as close to her as were her three younger sisters. In 1914, Prince Bernhard succeeded his father as reigning Duke of Saxe-Meiningen, but the reign of the new Duke and Duchess lasted only four years. In 1918, Bernhard abdicated, and one year later Charlotte died from cancer at the age of fifty-nine.

Prince Heinrich of Prussia

1862–1929

Vicky's third child, a second son, was born on 14 August, 1862, eight months after the death of her father, the Prince Consort, and it was therefore only to be expected that the child should be christened Albert. His other names were to be Wilhelm, after his paternal grandfather, and Heinrich. But although Queen Victoria would have liked her second grandson to be called by his first name, it was not to be. 'I had much wished we could have called baby "Albert",' Vicky told her, 'but as it would make so much confusion we shall be obliged to call him Henry.'

The birth had been remarkably easy, and the equable personality of the young prince seemed to reflect his effortless entry into the world. Vicky reported to her mother that Henry was 'such a sweet tempered child' and 'the cleverest of the three'.

It wasn't long, though, before the young prince proved a grievous disappointment to his mother. Like his elder brother and sister before him, Henry failed to live up to Vicky's high expectations, and she seized every opportunity to criticise his intelligence and appearance. 'I am sure you will like the poor child,' she wrote to her mother, shortly before four-year-old Henry set out on a visit to his grandmother at Windsor. 'He cannot help being so ugly, and he is really not stupid and can be very amusing.'

It was decided early on that Henry would have a career in the Navy, even though Queen Victoria did not think him strong enough. A model ship's mast, complete with sails, rigging and flags, was erected on the lawns behind the Neues Paleis, and Henry's great delight was to clamber up the rigging under the watchful gaze of a sailor. It soon became clear, though, that the prince was no scholar. When he was twelve, his mother complained that he was 'awfully backward in everything . . . is hopelessly lazy – dull and idle about his lessons.' The situation was no better two years later. 'His spelling and handwriting do not improve one bit, and he never reads – of his own accord!'

Prince Heinrich in 1873.

Prince Heinrich with his bride, Princess Irene of Hesse, shortly after their marriag in 1888. And (bottom) *Prince Heinrich in later life.*

Queen Victoria warned her daughter that no good would come of forcing Henry too much, and she was full of admiration for this second grandson, complimenting her on his nice manners.

Ten years later, when Henry had embarked on his naval career, he still won praise from his English grandmother: 'He is dear, simple and affectionate as ever, very fond of his profession.' She was less pleased four years after that when he fell in love with his first cousin, Princess Irene of Hesse, a daughter of his mother's sister, Alice. But Henry was determined to marry Irene, and the wedding finally took place on 24 May, 1888, Queen Victoria's birthday. Vicky was to remember it as 'by far the prettiest wedding we ever had', but the memories of other guests were tinged with sadness. Henry's father, now Emperor Friedrich III, was close to death from cancer of the throat. He was unable to speak and scarcely able to move but he left his sickbed to be present.

Henry and Irene set up their first home at Kiel, and Vicky visited them there as often as she could. Although she still criticised his lack of interest in books and the arts, her relationship with Henry was easier now that he was away from Berlin and the baleful influence of Wilhelm. By now Henry had become a Grand Admiral and was in command of the German fleet. When he was not away at sea, he amused himself with his collection of steam automobiles. Henry was among those who believed that steam was a more satisfactory method of propulsion than petrol, and his long-suffering family had to endure the discomfort of being blasted by intense heat and clouds of steam whenever they travelled in one of his vehicles.

Henry and Irene were a contented couple, popular with everyone and known to their relations as 'The Very Amiables'. A year after their wedding, Queen Victoria gave Henry the Order of the Garter because, by birth and by marriage, he was 'twice over my grandchild'. They were also liked by Edward VII, who made Prince Henry a Vice-Admiral of the British Fleet, and by his son, George V. Shortly before the First World War, Henry had a meeting with George and reported back to his brother the King's assurance that Britain would not come to the aid of France and Russia if they were attacked by Germany. Henry was later accused of deliberately misreporting the King's words, but he admitted that he had made a genuine mistake.

Such controversy, though, was rare in the lives of Prince Henry and his wife, who spent their final years peacefully at their estate in northern Germany. He died there in 1929, but Irene lived on until 1953.

Like her sister Alix, Irene was a carrier of haemophilia, and transmitted the disease to two of her three sons. The youngest, Heinrich, died of the disease at the age of four, but the eldest, Waldemar – known as Toddie – survived until 1945, when he died as a result of a shortage of blood transfusion facilities in the final months of the war. Henry's middle son, Sigismund, called Budgie by the family, led a normal, healthy life. In 1922 he left Germany to become a coffee grower in Guatemala. He died in Costa Rica in 1979.

Prince Heinrich's two eldest sons, Waldemar and Sigismund, in 1897. They were known in the family as Toddie and Budgie.

Prince Sigismund of Prussia 1864–1866

Prince Sigismund, the fourth child of Vicky and Fritz, was born on 11 September, 1864. Both parents doted on this young prince, who seemed so much more clever and intelligent than their other children. Vicky was even convinced that he would come to resemble her beloved father. But their pleasure was short-lived. Sigismund died from meningitis on 18 June, 1866, aged twenty-one months.

Vicky's grief and despair were intense. When the child fell ill, Fritz had been away from home, leading the Prussian forces into battle against Austria. He had taken all the available doctors with him to the front, and so Vicky was powerless to alleviate the suffering of her child or to prevent his death. She poured out her misery in letters to Queen Victoria: 'My pride, my joy, my hope, is gone, gone.' And, a few days later, 'Oh, to see it suffer so cruelly, to see it die and hear its last piteous cry – was an agony I cannot describe, it haunts me night and day!' The memory of Sigismund's death was to haunt Vicky for the rest of her life.

Prince Sigismund, pictured here with his mother in November 1865 (detail).

*The Crown Prince and Princess of
Prussia and their children in 1875.*
(Standing left to right) *Prince Heinrich,
Crown Princess Victoria, Crown Prince
Friedrich with Princess Margarete,
Prince Wilhelm and Princess Charlotte.*
(Seated left to right) *Princess Viktoria,
Princess Sophie and Prince Waldemar.*

Viktoria,
Princess Adolf of Schaumburg-Lippe
1866–1929

Princess Viktoria was born on 12 April, 1866, two months before the death of her brother, Sigismund. She was the second of Queen Victoria's granddaughters to be called by her name but, as was usual in the family, she was better known by her pet name, Moretta. Her childhood was spent agreeably enough in Berlin and Potsdam, and included many enjoyable visits to her doting grandmother at Windsor and Balmoral. Moretta grew into an extremely attractive young woman and it was assumed for a time that she would one day marry the son of the King of Portugal. This scheme was forgotten, though, when the reigning Prince of Bulgaria, Alexander of Battenberg, paid a state visit to Berlin in 1883.

Alexander had reigned in Bulgaria since 1879, a year after the new state was formed. Alexander's nomination as ruler had been proposed by the Tsar and by the German Emperor, but if the Tsar expected Alexander to be a puppet prince, he was sadly mistaken. Alexander – or Sandro, as he was known in royal circles – had no intention of being dominated by Russia, he assumed powers of dictatorship, and made it quite plain that he hoped to achieve complete independence for his new country.

These views did not endear Sandro to the Emperor or to the Tsar, and their approval was wearing thin at the time of his visit to Berlin. It was then that Sandro and Moretta met and fell in love, and in 1884 she and Sandro became engaged. Queen Victoria and Moretta's mother made no secret of their approval of the match.

This approval was not echoed by the Tsar, or by the German Emperor and Bismarck. They saw in this match an attempt by England to drive a wedge between Russia and Germany. The Battenberg family were altogether too friendly with Britain. One of Sandro's brothers was serving in the British Navy, and another was married to Queen Victoria's youngest daughter, Beatrice.

Vicky and Sandro retreated in the face of this opposition, and it was

Princess Viktoria as a young woman. Her mother said of her 'She has such a sweet disposition. I shall never feel anxious on her account, if she is but spared!'

Princess Viktoria with two animal friends. This princess seemed destined for a glittering future but no one could have foreseen that her first love affair would provoke an international confrontation.

secretly agreed that the engagement should be kept in suspended animation until the ailing Emperor died. The situation would be different when Fritz assumed the German throne. Sandro returned to Bulgaria, where he divided his time between antagonising the Tsar and writing copious letters to Moretta and her mother. From England Sandro received letters of support from Queen Victoria: 'I must follow the impulse of my heart,' she wrote, 'and tell you how warm and fervent my sympathy and prayers have been for you.'

Such encouragement may have strengthened Sandro's resolve, but it could not prevent the Tsar from taking drastic action. In 1886, he arranged for Sandro to be kidnapped from his palace in Sofia and imprisoned in Russia. The Prince was freed two weeks later, but this humiliation ended any possibility of continuing his rule in Bulgaria. He abdicated and returned to his home in Hesse.

In 1888, the old Emperor died and Fritz ascended the German throne. The chances of the marriage taking place now seemed more promising, but Bismarck was still determined to prevent it. Moretta's brother Wilhelm, now crown prince and future emperor, shared Bismarck's view.

It was now five years since that first meeting in Berlin, and Sandro's devotion began to wilt under the strain of such prolonged separation and controversy. In 1889, he fell in love with a beautiful opera singer, Johanna Loisinger, and decided to marry her instead.

Moretta tried as best she could to forget the past. The natural course of action was to follow Sandro's example and get married, but any other prince could only be second best. Even so, Vicky and Queen Victoria scoured the courts of Europe for a suitable husband. Two

Russian grand dukes and a prince of Anhalt were considered and discarded and then, in June 1890, Vicky was able to tell her daughter Sophie that Moretta was engaged to Prince Adolf of Schaumburg-Lippe. It was clear, though, that the prince was disappointing. Stiff, shy, awkward – poor Adolf was in striking contrast to the handsome, brave and charming Sandro.

Adolf loved Moretta, but her feelings for him were less enthusiastic, and she was critical of much about him – his beard, his clothes and his servants. But the marriage took place at the end of the year and, after a honeymoon in Italy and Egypt, Moretta and Adolf took up residence in the Schaumburg Palace in Bonn.

Moretta was deeply affected by Sandro's premature death in 1893. With Sandro gone, and no prospect of children, she resigned herself to a dull and dismal future. In 1916 Adolf died and she was left alone in the vast palace in Bonn. The First World War brought some excitement into Moretta's life, even though this was confined to economising on food and foregoing the luxuries that she took for granted.

As peace returned to Germany, Moretta became increasingly lonely, eccentric and odd. And then, in 1927, she met Alexander Zoubkoff. He was a handsome young man who claimed to be of noble Russian blood, but who was forced to work as a waiter because his family fortunes had vanished in the Revolution. Moretta believed this story, and all the other lies he told her. She was fair game for the smooth and unscrupulous Zoubkoff. He flattered her, praised her and said that he loved her. At the end of the year they were married.

Moretta wrote afterwards, 'It is surprising to me that a matter so private and personal as one's own marriage should become so public that the world must seize upon it and treat it as a matter of widespread interest.' But one could hardly blame the world for showing some curiosity. Moretta was sixty-one when she married, and Zoubkoff was only twenty-seven. Moreover, Moretta was the Kaiser's sister, a royal princess of considerable wealth, and Zoubkoff was a penniless nonentity.

The marriage to Zoubkoff was a final desperate attempt to find the happiness that had always eluded her. But in this, as in her love for Sandro and her marriage to Adolf, she was to be disappointed. After a few months Zoubkoff deserted her, taking with him all that remained of her fortune. Moretta did not long survive the humiliation of seeing her property and possessions being sold at public auction to pay her creditors. In 1929 she died, alone, embittered and abandoned by most of her family.

Viktoria and Alexander Zoubkoff at the time of their wedding in 1927. 'People will say that there is too great a difference in our ages for complete happiness,' she declared, 'but if two people really care for each other nothing else matters.'

Prince Waldemar of Prussia
1868–1879

Prince Waldemar aged five, and (top) *shortly before his death in 1879.*

The birth of Prince Waldemar on 10 February, 1868, helped to fill the gap left in Vicky's life by the death of Sigismund two years earlier. He was born on Queen Victoria's wedding anniversary, and so it was only to be expected that once again the Queen would express strong views about the choice of appropriate names for her latest grandson. She hoped that the young prince would be called Victor Albert, but his parents had already decided on Joachim Friedrich Ernst Waldemar and felt that two more names would be a little too much.

Waldemar was to become the favourite son of both Vicky and Fritz. Unlike his brothers, he was quick to learn and his mother found him a pleasure to teach. But although the prince was more gifted than his brothers, he was no bookworm; he was boisterous and high-spirited, with a sensible, independent and honest nature that delighted his parents. Vicky always claimed that he resembled her father, but although the prince may have shared his grandfather's intelligence, Waldemar's extrovert, fun-loving character was quite different from that of the Prince Consort.

On 24 March, 1879, Prince Waldemar fell ill with diphtheria, and three days later he was dead. Vicky mourned him as 'the dearest, nicest and most promising' of her sons, and this death, coming so soon after the deaths from diphtheria of her sister Alice and niece Marie, spurred her to investigate the causes of the disease and the reasons for its prevalence in Germany, where the death rate was so much higher than in England. Although she correctly identified poor drains as the source of the infection, it would be another fifteen years before medical science finally solved the mystery.

Sophie, Queen of Greece
1870–1932

Sophie was her mother's favourite. When she was born in 1870, Queen Victoria, as always, had disapproved strongly of the name of the young princess, thinking it ugly. As it turned out, this hardly mattered because Vicky invariably addressed her daughter by a variety of nicknames: Fozzie, Sossie, Sosikin, Sophiekin. Ludicrous pet names were commonplace in royal circles, but Princess Sophie had more than her fair share.

Shortly after her father's death, Sophie became engaged to Prince Constantine, the eldest son of King George I of Greece. This match received the wholehearted approval of Queen Victoria and of Wilhelm, who managed to convince himself that he alone had arranged it for political reasons. Although Vicky was fond of Prince Constantine – or Tino, as he was known in the family – she did have some doubts about the marriage. The Greek throne was very insecure, and the country was underdeveloped and primitive. But the spectacular wedding took place as arranged in October 1889, in the presence of a large gathering of what Queen Victoria always called 'the royal mob'.

Despite Vicky's misgivings, Sophie settled happily to her new life. Court life in Athens was much more informal than in Berlin; there were far fewer social distinctions and little formal entertaining. Sophie and Tino lived in an unpretentious villa where they cultivated a calm domestic atmosphere that was almost entirely English. They spoke English to one another, and employed English nannies, governesses and doctors for their growing family. Sophie and Tino were to have six children; each of their sons was to be king of Greece and, of their three daughters, two would be queens and the youngest would marry an English commoner.

Sophie depended on her mother for help and encouragement, and Vicky was only too glad to provide advice on everything from child-rearing and buying furniture to gardening and drains. Sophie's interests were centred almost entirely on her family, and her mother

Queen Sophie of Greece. Her natural reserve often made her appear cold and unapproachable.

Sophie and Constantine at breakfast in the Royal Palace, Athens, in 1913. From left to right, Princess Irene, Prince George, Queen Sophie with Princess Katherine, King Constantine, Princess Helen, Prince Alexander and Prince Paul.

was often irritated by her apparent lack of interest in politics or the social welfare of the Greek people. As the years passed, though, the shy, insecure princess grew into a forceful woman of great dignity and strength of character, although her natural reserve often made her appear unapproachable.

Sophie's domestic life with her children and the charming Tino may have been harmonious, but events elsewhere were not. In 1891, Sophie was received into the Greek Orthodox Church, a move that appalled her brother, the Kaiser. He banished her from Germany and refused to speak to her again.

Sophie's life at home was not without its complications either. In 1913 King George was assassinated by a lunatic while he was out for a walk, and Tino became King Constantine I. He was highly popular at first, thanks to his success in the Balkan Wars against Turkey and Bulgaria, but the mood of the Greek government and people fluctuated alarmingly in the years that followed. When the First World War broke out in 1914, Tino was determined that Greece should remain neutral. The Prime Minister and the Allied powers were equally determined that Greece should side against Germany. The King was accused of being pro-German, and it was naturally assumed that Queen Sophie supported her brother, the Kaiser. Wild rumours abounded, and a disastrous fire was deliberately started at the royal estate of Tatoi with the intention of killing the King and Queen. It was only after an Allied blockade turned the mood of the people against him that Tino agreed to leave the country as the government demanded. But he refused to sign an act of abdication before leaving with Sophie for lonely exile in Switzerland.

Constantine as Crown Prince of Greece.

Sophie and Tino's eldest son, George, was also thought to have pro-German leanings and so it was their second son, Alexander, who now became king. But his reign was brief. Sophie was disturbed by his morganatic marriage in 1919 to Aspasia Manos, the daughter of one of Tino's equerries, but worse news was to come. A year later, Alexander died suddenly after being bitten by a pet monkey. The crown was next offered to Sophie's third son, Paul, but when he refused it, the new government organised a plebiscite on the monarchy. The people decided that Tino should be asked to come back, and he and Sophie returned to Athens in 1920 amid scenes of wild enthusiasm.

Their stay was to be a short one. The mood of the people changed yet again after the failure of a military campaign against Turkey, and, in 1922, Tino and Sophie were forced into exile once more. This time their departure was permanent. Tino abdicated, and the crown passed to George. A few weeks later, Tino died in Palermo from a brain haemorrhage.

The Greek government refused to allow Tino to be buried in Greece and so Sophie arranged for his interment in the crypt of the Russian Orthodox church in Florence, where she was to spend the last years of her life. She died of cancer in 1932.

Crown Princess Sophie with her children. From left to right, Princess Helen, Prince Paul (front), *Princess Irene, Prince George* (back) *and Prince Alexander.*

Margarete, Landgravine of Hesse
1872–1954

Princess Margarete, right, with her sister, Princess Sophie, in August 1882.

With the marriage of her two elder sisters, Princess Margarete was left alone with her mother. Fortunately Vicky did not share the views of Queen Victoria, who believed that it was the duty of a youngest daughter to remain at home as a companion to her mother, and she was determined that Margarete – known as Mossy – should marry as well as possible. Mossy was not as attractive as Moretta or Sophie, but her mother once described her as 'such a love, such a little sunbeam, so good and so gifted', and this amiable and charming princess seemed destined to make a brilliant royal marriage. Indeed, Queen Victoria hinted to her grandson, the Duke of Clarence, that Mossy would make both an ideal bride for him and a perfect queen, but the princess only had eyes for handsome, dashing Prince Max of Baden. Sadly, her infatuation for this prince was not reciprocated, and he married a princess of Hanover instead.

And then, in 1892, Vicky was able to report to Queen Victoria that Mossy had become engaged to Prince Friedrich Karl of Hesse, or Fischy, as he was known in royal circles for some reason. Vicky was delighted with the match, for the prince was humorous, cultivated and well-read, and had a great deal in common with his future mother-in-law. There were drawbacks, however. Fischy was not rich and he had no property of his own. Mossy's brother, Wilhelm, was not alone in considering this poor, insignificant prince an unequal match for an Emperor's sister but, even so, he loftily informed Mossy that he was prepared to give his consent to the marriage because she was so unimportant.

Princess Margarete occupies a unique position in recent royal history because she gave birth to two sets of twin boys, Philipp and Wolfgang in 1896, and Richard and Christoph in 1901. (They had been preceded by two single sons, Friedrich Wilhelm in 1893 and Maximilian in 1894.) When the first set of twins was born, one of Queen Victoria's ladies-in-waiting noted that 'the Queen laughed very much and is rather amused at the list of her great-grandchildren being added to in such a rapid manner.'

Mossy and Fischy were a quiet and popular pair, and Mossy in particular was noted for her loyalty and kindness to her family and friends. Her later years, though, were darkened by tragedy. Both her elder sons were killed in action during the First World War, and Prince Christoph, a major in the Luftwaffe, died while on active service in the Second World War. He was married to Princess Sophie of Greece, a sister of Prince Philip, Duke of Edinburgh. Both Prince Christoph and Prince Philipp of Hesse were ardent Nazis, and Prince Philipp, at one time the lover of the English poet Siegfried Sassoon, achieved notoriety when he acted as an intermediary between Mussolini and Hitler. He was married to Princess Mafalda of Italy, who was imprisoned in Buchenwald concentration camp when her father, King Vittorio Emanuele III capitulated to the Allies in 1943. She died there a year later. Another of Mossy's daughters-in-law, Prince Wolfgang's wife Marie-Alexandra of Baden, was killed in an air raid the same year.

Mossy had inherited her mother's home, Schloss Friedrichshof, and it was there that another drama took place at the end of the Second World War. Shortly before the castle was occupied by American troops, Mossy concealed her jewels in one of the cellars for safe keeping. The castle was used as an officers' club and the manager discovered the jewels, stole them, and smuggled them out of Germany with the help of two officers. When the princess discovered the theft the culprits were traced and imprisoned, but most of the jewellery was never recovered.

Mossy lived on until 1954. Apart from the tragic death of her sons and daughters-in-law, her life had been peaceful and free of controversy. In 1918 though, this quiet unpretentious princess had very nearly become a queen. When Finland achieved independence from Russia after the Revolution, Mossy's husband, Friedrich Karl, was elected King of Finland by the country's parliament. The new king told the Finnish people that he wished to await the result of the peace negotiations before accepting the throne, and withdrew his candidature on 20 December, 1918, after a 'reign' of just two months. The Finnish government did not look elsewhere for a monarch; instead the country became a republic. It would have been a strange twist of fate if the prince who had been thought an unsuitable husband for the Kaiser's sister had become a king after all.

Princess Margarete after her marriage to Prince Friedrich Karl of Hesse. She was noted for her loyalty to family and friends.

The Children of Edward and Alexandra

Albert Victor
Duke of Clarence
1864–1892

George V
King of Great Britain
1865–1936

Louise
Duchess of Fife
1867–1931

Victoria
Princess of Great Britain
1868–1935

Maud
Queen of Norway
1869–1938

John
Prince of Great Britain
1871

Edward VII 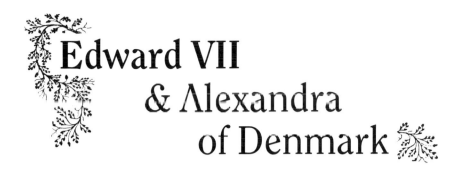 & Alexandra of Denmark

The birth of Victoria's first son in 1841 came only eleven and a half months after that of his sister. He was named after his father, but known in the family as Bertie.

Although Bertie was so close to Vicky in age, they were completely different in character and temperament. He was lazy, slow and reluctant to learn, and he did not have the mental or emotional ability to match his parents' expectations. Albert hoped to mould his son as a model constitutional monarch, and so he was isolated from boys of his own age and subjected to a rigorous schedule of instruction. His parents became increasingly disappointed at Bertie's progress, and their hopes were finally destroyed by the scandal of his love affair with Nelly Clifden. Queen Victoria was convinced that the shock of this discovery precipitated Prince Albert's death from typhoid a few weeks later, and she never forgave her son.

The grieving Queen decided that Bertie should be married as soon as possible and a match was arranged with the beautiful Princess Alexandra of Denmark. The Queen then withdrew completely from public life, leaving Bertie to perform ceremonial duties, but keeping him in complete ignorance of the business of government.

During his long years as Prince of Wales, Bertie became the most fashionable figure in European society. Fun-loving, affectionate, gregarious and generous, Bertie delighted in the company of financiers and beautiful women. He adored his children, and happily tolerated their wild behaviour, while Alexandra made up for her husband's absences and infidelities by smothering the children with a possessive, obsessive love which left them shy, immature and shallow.

When Bertie at last became King in 1901 he was nearly sixty, but his brief reign restored the ceremonial aspects of the monarchy and his court became the most splendid in Europe. He died in 1910, but Alexandra lived a further twenty years, retaining her legendary beauty well into old age.

Edward and Alexandra with their children: George (standing left), *Victoria* (standing right) *and, seated left to right, Maud, Albert Victor and Louise.*

Albert Victor, Duke of Clarence
1864–1892

Although Prince Albert Victor of Wales was not the first of Queen Victoria's grandchildren he was, at the time of his birth, by far the most significant. As the eldest son of the Prince of Wales, it was he who would one day inherit the throne of Great Britain. Queen Victoria did not hesitate to decide that the child should be named Albert Victor. The first that Bertie heard of this decision was when his six-year-old sister Beatrice told him. 'I felt rather annoyed,' he wrote to his mother. As it was, Bertie and Alexandra had already planned to name their son Edward and so he was always known to the family as Eddy.

The birth of the young prince was two months premature. His arrival in January 1864 took everyone by surprise and was to have a disastrous effect on his health and vigour. From the first, he was delicate and slow to develop. Nothing seemed to interest him, and he was very slow to learn. The Prince of Wales was irritated by Eddy's feebleness, but the boy was adored by his mother and idolised by his younger sisters, and his pampered and undisciplined upbringing was to give rise to a dissipated self-indulgent life-style when he was older.

The differences between Eddy and his younger brother, George, could not have been more marked. Whereas Eddy was languid and listless, George was active and high-spirited. So, although George was destined for a naval career and Eddy was not, it was considered that separation from his brother would cause Eddy more harm than good and both he and George went to Dartmouth as naval cadets. Eddy then spent some time at Trinity College, Cambridge, followed by a period in the army, but neither of these experiences helped to invigorate his mind or character. It was becoming abundantly clear that Prince Eddy was completely unsuited to the high position that he would one day inherit.

The prince's private life was also giving rise to concern. In 1889, his name was linked with those of several aristocrats discovered to have frequented a male brothel in London. The Prince of Wales's friend,

Albert Victor (right) *with his younger brother, George. They were devoted to each other and it was decided that they should be educated together.*

Princess Alexandra with her eldest sons, Albert Victor and George (above) *and Albert Victor alone* (right).

Lord Arthur Somerset, was implicated in the scandal and it was said that it was he who introduced Eddy to the notorious establishment in Cleveland Street. But there is no evidence that Eddy was homosexual or even bisexual.

It was extraordinary rumours like these which so alarmed the Prince of Wales and convinced him that drastic action was needed to solve the problem of Prince Eddy. It was proposed that Eddy should either be dispatched abroad, or else be married immediately to a strong-minded princess. The first alternative was quickly dismissed as being likely to offer too many opportunities for further licentious behaviour, and it was decided instead that Eddy should marry.

Eddy had his own answer to this question: he had fallen in love with his beautiful cousin, Princess Alix of Hesse. This match seemed entirely suitable, but the fiercely independent Alix did not agree. Queen Victoria was disappointed by her decision ('She refuses the greatest position there is'), but she was full of admiration for her granddaughter's determination.

Eddy did not long regret the loss of Alix. Within a week he had fallen in love with another princess, Hélène of Orléans. This match, though, was completely unsuitable. Princess Hélène was the second daughter of the Comte de Paris, Pretender to the throne of France, and the princess was Roman Catholic; marriage with the heir to the British throne was out of the question. Despite these objections, the romance prospered, thanks to the active support of Princess Alexandra and Eddy's sister, Princess Louise. Soon Queen Victoria's opposition changed to sympathy, and a series of discussions ensued on the constitutional implications of the heir apparent marrying a Roman Catholic princess. Eddy declared that he was prepared to renounce his right of succession to the throne, but Hélène's father refused to allow her to marry a Protestant. The romance withered in the face of these obstacles, and by the spring of 1891 it was over.

Towards the end of 1891, the problem of Prince Albert Victor's marriage was solved, at last, when he proposed to Princess Mary of Teck. Princess Mary – or May as she was known in the family – was the only daughter of Queen Victoria's first cousin, Princess Mary Adelaide of Cambridge. Quiet, conscientious, well-educated, unsel-

Princess Hélène d'Orléans, whose romance with Prince Albert Victor was encouraged by his mother and his sister, Louise. He was to cry out her name over and over again during his final illness.

Albert Victor and George as naval cadets (left). Their training included a cruise round the world in which their vessel narrowly escaped shipwreck. Albert Victor later joined the 10th Hussars and is seen below in his uniform, with members of his staff.

Prince Albert Victor photographed as a country gentleman. He was often called 'Collar-and-Cuffs' behind his back, for reasons which are easily apparent.

Prince Albert Victor with Princess May of Teck, taken soon after their engagement in 1891.

fish, intelligent, well travelled – May was an ideal bride for any prince. But, ironically enough, even the most minor German princeling would have refused to contemplate marriage with her. May's father, the Duke of Teck, was the son of Duke Alexander of Württemberg and his morganatic wife, Countess Rhédey von Kis-Rhéde, and therefore not of full royal rank. Happily, Queen Victoria had no time for such genealogical niceties. She knew May would be a highly suitable bride for Eddy. Sadly, the Queen's enlightened views were not shared by all her royal relatives, but Eddy seemed genuinely fond of May, and she was certainly in love with him. The wedding was therefore arranged for 27 February, 1892.

On 7 January, 1892, a month after the engagement was announced, Eddy complained of feeling unwell while out shooting at Sandringham. He was diagnosed as suffering from influenza, and in the days that followed the illness developed into pneumonia. In the early morning of 14 January, Prince Albert Victor died.

The royal family and the country were grieved and stunned by the suddenness of Eddy's death. The tragedy of the young prince dying so unexpectedly on the eve of his wedding created a public sensation. It had to be admitted that his death came as a blessing in disguise. He was totally unsuited to be king and, even with the support and guidance of a consort as sensible and forthright as Princess May, the future course of the British monarchy would have been bleak and unpredictable had he succeeded to the throne.

After Eddy's death, his adored brother, George, became heir apparent, and the attention of the nation turned to this handsome, likeable young prince. And there was someone else, too, who excited the nation's sympathy and curiosity – the romantic figure of the grieving Princess May.

George V, King of Great Britain
1865–1936

The life of Prince George of Wales changed dramatically on the death of his elder brother. Until then it had been assumed that he would make a career in the Navy, and that he would lead a quiet life out of the public eye. All this changed with Eddy's death. George was now the heir apparent, and the prospect was daunting.

Once again the attention of the Queen and her family turned to the interesting problem of finding a suitable consort for a future King of Great Britain. George himself had hoped to marry his beautiful, fascinating cousin, Marie, the eldest daughter of Prince Alfred, Duke of Edinburgh, but the princess, with characteristic wilfulness, had turned him down, much to George's disappointment, and the irritation of the Prince of Wales, who felt that his son had been snubbed.

It soon became apparent to all that an ideal answer to the problem lay close at hand. Princess May of Teck had been considered an ideal bride for Eddy and a suitable future queen of Great Britain. There seemed, therefore, to be no good reason why she should not marry George instead. The only obstacle to this perfect solution lay with the young couple themselves. Both George and May were distressed and embarrassed by the situation that confronted them. They had both been devoted to Eddy and it was this shared grief, rather than any physical attraction, that now drew them together. Nevertheless their friendship developed into respect and affection, and sixteen months after Eddy's death, George proposed to May. She accepted, and the nation breathed a sigh of relief. George and May were married in great splendour in July 1893; all of May's ten bridesmaids were grand-daughters of Queen Victoria, and of these at least two would have liked to have been in the bride's place themselves.

Although to the world at large George may have appeared shy and inarticulate, he was by far the most attractive of the children of the Prince of Wales in both appearance and character. As a child he was dutiful but high-spirited, and was once described by a family friend as

The Princess of Wales with Prince George, aged one, in 1866.

(Above left) *The Princess of Wales with Prince Albert Victor* (left) *and Prince George at Abergeldie, near Balmoral, in 1866.* (Above right) *Prince Albert Victor and Prince George, dressed as Scottish country gentlemen.*

being a 'jolly little pickle'. It is said that he was once so naughty that Queen Victoria made him sit under the dining table until he promised to be good. When at last she gave him permission to emerge, he appeared stark naked, much to the amusement of his grandmother and her guests. The prince was devoted to his mother, as she was to him, and to the end of his life he spoke of her as being the most beautiful woman in the world. Even as an adult George would begin his letters to her with 'My own darling sweet little beloved Motherdear' and sign himself 'Your loving little George'. Her letters to him were equally fulsome, often closing with the phrase, 'With a great big kiss for your lovely little face.'

George was no scholar, and to the end of his life he remained indifferent to art and history, had little understanding of science and politics, and never learned a foreign language. But he excelled at seamanship, and during his naval training he mastered Practical Navigation and other technical subjects. His great enthusiasms were shooting and stamp collecting. Even by the standards of his day, George's addiction to the slaughter of game birds was quite extraordinary. It is recorded that on one single day at Sandringham, George fired 1700 cartridges and brought down 1000 pheasants. Even so he would have been deeply shocked if anyone had doubted his fondness for animals and birds. His legendary stamp collection had been started by his uncle, Prince Alfred, Duke of Edinburgh, who later sold it to the

Prince of Wales. The Prince then passed it to George, who built it up over the years until it became the most comprehensive collection in the world of the stamps of Great Britain and her colonies and dependencies.

George and May were to have six children. When their first son was born in 1894, Queen Victoria was quick to make known her views on the choice of name. She was anxious that the prince should be called Albert, as she wished all future kings of the dynasty to bear this name. (After Eddy's death she had even tried to persuade George to use his last name, Albert, instead.) George told his grandmother that he and May wished their son to be called Edward, after his dead brother. Queen Victoria promptly replied that Eddy's name had, in fact, been Albert Victor, not Edward, but George remained adamant. In the end, the young prince was always known in the family by his last name, David, although he was to reign briefly as King Edward VIII. It was this son who was to cause his parents such unhappiness when he was

(Below left) 'Motherdear' with her children. (Back row, left to right) Prince Albert Victor, Princess Alexandra, Princess Victoria, Prince George. (Front) Princess Louise and Princess Maud. (Below right) Prince George with his sisters, Victoria, Maud and (seated) Louise.

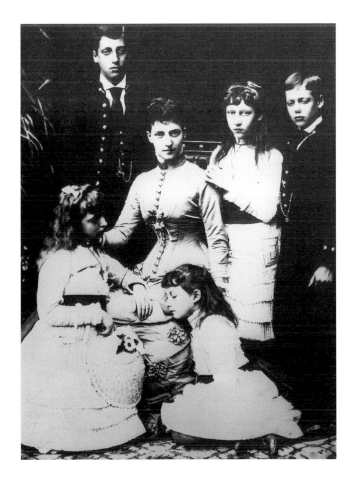

The wedding of Prince George and Princess May of Teck in 1893. The bridesmaids were (back row, left to right) Princess Alexandra of Edinburgh, Princess Helena Victoria of Schleswig-Holstein, Princess Victoria Melita of Edinburgh, Princess Victoria of Wales, Princess Maud of Wales. (Middle row) Princess Alice of Battenberg, Princess Margaret of Connaught. (Front row) Princess Beatrice of Edinburgh, Princess Ena of Battenberg, Princess Patricia of Connaught.

older. As Prince of Wales, David displayed a wilful disregard for their wishes in his dress, duty and behaviour, but it was May alone who was to suffer the pain of his relationship with Mrs Simpson and the abdication crisis that followed.

George's relationship with his other sons was more harmonious. Prince Albert, born in 1895, married Lady Elizabeth Bowes-Lyon in 1923 and reigned as King George VI, until his death in 1952 and the succession of Queen Elizabeth II. Prince Henry, Duke of Gloucester, married Lady Alice Montagu-Douglas-Scott and died in 1974. His brother, George, Duke of Kent, was killed in an air crash in 1942 while on active service. He was the only one of King George V's sons to marry a royal princess, Marina of Greece and Denmark. Prince John, born in 1905, was epileptic and died in 1919.

May had hoped that their only daughter, Mary, born in 1897, would marry Prince Ernst August of Brunswick, but he married the daughter of Kaiser Wilhelm II instead, and the First World War put an end to any further thoughts of a German marriage. Instead, Princess Mary was married in 1928 to Viscount Lascelles, later Earl of Harewood, who was fifteen years her senior. She was created Princess Royal in 1932 and died in 1965.

On 6 May, 1910, King Edward VII died and George became King. 'I have lost my best friend and the best of fathers,' he wrote in his diary. The character of the new King was very different from that of his father, but with wise counsel from experienced advisors and his own blend of kindliness and commonsense he was to prove a sensible and popular monarch.

His reign spanned nearly thirty years of unparalleled political and technical change. The First World War and the downfall of the empires of Russia, Germany and Austria; demands for Irish Home Rule and Indian self-government; the decline of the House of Lords, the rise of the Labour Party and the General Strike of 1926 – all these events were to transform the lives of the King and his people.

His family, too, was not immune to change. Even though he considered himself to be completely British, the German ancestry of George and May provoked rumours that they did not wholeheartedly support the Allied cause in the First World War. George took drastic steps to restore the nation's confidence in his patriotism. In 1917, he changed the name of the dynasty to the House of Windsor, and declared that all members of the royal family should relinquish all 'German degrees, styles, dignities, titles, honours and appellations.' And so, overnight, His Serene Highness Prince Louis of Battenberg became the Marquess of Milford Haven, and Queen Mary's brother, Prince Alexander of Teck, became the Earl of Athlone. Other members of the family exchanged Battenberg for Mountbatten and Teck for Cambridge. At the same time, the King regulated and defined the future use of princely titles so as to avoid the proliferation of princes and princesses that occurred in foreign royal families.

Although his views may have been reactionary and old-fashioned, King George V was able to adapt to a changing world, and he had no difficulty working with a Labour government. And, as the thrones of his cousins toppled into oblivion, the King's calm domestic life and strong sense of duty kept the British monarchy secure for future generations.

(Above) *The familiar image of King George V, taken in 1907.* (Below) *The King inspecting the Irish Division in 1915.*

Louise, Duchess of Fife

1867–1931

(Above) *The young Princess Louise, and* (below) *the Princess with her husband, the Duke of Fife.*

Princess Louise, the eldest daughter of the Prince and Princess of Wales, was born on 20 February, 1867. Alexandra developed rheumatic fever shortly before the birth and for a time it was thought that her life was in danger. Happily, both mother and child survived, but the illness left Alexandra with a permanently stiff knee (the 'Alexandra limp' was later to become fashionable), and brought on hereditary deafness that was to plague her for the rest of her life.

The childhood of Princess Louise was unusually informal; her father was jovial and sociable by nature and he was determined that his own children should be allowed the freedom, enjoyment and fun that had been denied him when he was young. The result was a brood of unruly youngsters who presented an inhibited and retiring face to the world (Louise and her sisters were known behind their backs as 'Their Royal Shynesses'), but were quite the opposite in private. Queen Victoria once described them as being 'such ill-bred, ill-trained children, I can't fancy them at all'.

The children were the focus of Alexandra's life and, by depriving them of the realities of the outside world, she hoped to make them dependent upon her for as long as possible. In this she succeeded. In private, the Wales princesses behaved like children long after they had reached adulthood, and Princess Louise even celebrated her nineteenth birthday with a children's party. In public, though, she was painfully shy, and found conversation with strangers almost impossible. Even after her marriage, she refused to join family parties at Balmoral and kept her own children apart from their closest relations.

When she was twenty-two, Louise was married to the Earl of Fife, who was eighteen years her senior. The match caused controversy among her relations; it was felt by some that a future Princess Royal should marry a royal prince and not a commoner. Queen Victoria did not share these misgivings, mainly because the bridegroom was immensely rich, owning fourteen country houses and more than

100,000 acres, though none of these were in Fife. The Queen created him Duke of Fife shortly after the wedding, which took place on 27 July, 1889 at Buckingham Palace.

After her marriage, Princess Louise led a retired life as far from the public gaze as she could manage. Her only real interest was fishing, but she was also a talented amateur musician. Louise was to have two daughters of her own, both of whom were given the title Princess by their grandfather in 1905, when Louise was created Princess Royal. Princess Alexandra became a trained nurse and, after working at University College Hospital as 'Nurse Marjorie', founded her own nursing home in London. She married her mother's cousin, Prince Arthur of Connaught, in 1913, and became Duchess of Fife in her own right after her father's death. Her sister, Princess Maud, enjoyed country pursuits and shared her mother's passion for fishing. In 1923 she married the Earl of Southesk, who is still living.

In 1911, Princess Louise became the reluctant participant in a dramatic rescue at sea when the ship on which she and her husband and daughters were travelling to Egypt ran aground and sank off the Moroccan coast. Their lifeboat also sank, and the royal survivors were forced to float in the water in lifebelts until they were rescued. Their ordeal continued after they reached land. Suffering from cold and shock, they were forced to walk five miles before they reached the mules that then carried them a further ten miles to Tangier. The royal party then continued on their journey to Egypt, where they were going for the sake of Princess Louise's delicate health. Ironically enough, it was not the Princess who succumbed from this experience but her husband, the Duke of Fife, who contracted pleurisy and died at Aswan during their visit.

Princess Louise spent the remaining twenty years of her life in retirement at her London house in Portman Square, and by the time of her death in 1931 she had been largely forgotten by the public at large.

(From left to right) *The Duke and Duchess of Fife with their first child, Alexandra, and the Duke and Duchess with Alexandra and her younger sister, Maud. They were both granted the title Princess by their grandfather in 1905.*

(Right) *Princess Louise,*
Princess Maud and
Princess Victoria with their
maternal grandmother,
Queen Louise of Denmark,
in 1882. (Below left)
Princess Victoria with her
bicycle, and (right) Victoria
and Maud as bridesmaids
at the wedding of their sister
Louise in 1889.

Princess Victoria

1868–1935

The marriage of Princess Louise in 1889 left her sisters, Victoria and Maud, alone with their doting mother at Sandringham. The two princesses were hardly ever seen apart, and they looked and even dressed alike. Of the two sisters, it was Victoria who was regarded as being the liveliest and most intelligent, and she was certainly her aunt's favourite. 'That dear Victoria is an angel of a girl,' she wrote to her daughter, Sophie, 'so good and unselfish, so helpful, useful and true. Of all the nieces I have, I love her the best.'

These sentiments were certainly shared by Victoria's mother, who was determined that this 'helpful, useful and true' daughter should never leave home. Both Victoria and Maud found themselves trapped in a gilded cage by a fond mother who prevented any attempt to escape.

When she was young, however, there was every prospect that Princess Victoria would make a splendid marriage. It was felt that this intelligent, attractive daughter of the future King Edward VII would make an ideal bride for some ambitious prince. But Alexandra blocked every attempt at matchmaking. The Prince of Wales hoped that Victoria might marry Prince Adolphus of Teck, the charming brother of Princess May, but Princess Alexandra spurned this suggestion on the grounds that Prince Dolly was not sufficiently royal.

As the years passed, rumour linked Princess Victoria's name with other, less distinguished suitors, including Sir Arthur Davidson, one of her father's equerries. And there is evidence to suggest that Lord Rosebery, the future Prime Minister, wished to marry Victoria and asked the Prince of Wales for her hand. Although Rosebery was twenty years older than the princess, and a widower with grown-up children, it seems that his affection for her was genuine and deeply-felt. He was an ambitious politician and therefore well aware of the disadvantages to his career of a close relationship with the throne but, even so, he persisted with his suit. However, the startled Prince of

Princess Victoria as a young woman. Her aunt Vicky thought her 'an angel of a girl,' but others suffered from her sharp tongue.

As she grew older, Princess Victoria developed a fondness for making mischief and meddling in the lives of her relations. Her nephew, King Edward VIII, remembered her as 'a bitch of the first order.'

Wales would not hear of it, fearing a threat to the monarchy from so close a link with Liberal Party politics. Princess Victoria returned Rosebery's affection and bitterly resented her parents' opposition to their marriage. In later life, she would speak sadly of this rejection of a man who would have been perfect for her, adding that they '*could* have been so happy.'

In 1896, Princess Maud at last succeeded in breaking free when she married Prince Carl of Denmark. Victoria was now left quite alone with her mother, and she would remain at her beck and call for the next thirty years. As time passed, Alexandra became increasingly tyrannical, keeping a special bell by her side with which to summon her daughter at any time of day or night. The Grand Duchess Olga, sister of Tsar Nicholas II, remembered Victoria as being little more than 'a glorified maid', forced to interrupt whatever she might be doing at the sound of her mother's bell. It is hardly surprising that she soon became known in the family as 'poor Toria'.

Even as a girl Victoria was noted for her sharp tongue, and this characteristic grew more pronounced as the years passed. Princess May, the wife of her brother, George, was the frequent victim of her verbal attacks. She once told a guest, 'Now do try and talk to May at dinner, though one knows she is deadly dull.' Like her mother and sisters, Victoria was contemptuous of May's morganatic blood and jealous of her superior intelligence and artistic interests. When, shortly after her mother's death, she joined George and May on a cruise round the Mediterranean, Victoria ruined the holiday for May by constantly mocking her love of beauty and antiquity, and by encouraging her brother to join in these attacks. 'I am glad to be back,' May wrote with relief on her return.

Victoria's other preoccupation was her health. Neuralgia, constant influenza, migraines, digestive difficulties, perpetual colds, depression – these and other ailments kept Princess Victoria increasingly occupied as she grew older. Although she was generally disliked, the princess could show affection when she chose. She was very fond of her nephew, the Duke of Kent, and bequeathed her Buckinghamshire home to him. And she was devoted to her brother, George. He, in his turn, was deeply attached to her. The King was so distressed by her death in 1935 that he cancelled the State Opening of Parliament. For the first time in his life, he felt unable to face his public duties. 'No one ever had a sister like her,' he wrote in his diary. The King did not appear in public again, and he died two months later.

Maud, Queen of Norway

1869–1938

None of the daughters of Edward and Alexandra inherited the exceptional beauty of their mother. But it was the youngest, Princess Maud, who was the most attractive and, consequently, her father's favourite.

Maud was more determined and rebellious than her sisters, and it was she who accused their mother, when they were older, of not doing enough to arrange marriages for them. Then she took the law into her own hands by falling in love with Prince Francis of Teck, the brother of Princess May. Sadly, Prince Frank was a highly unsuitable candidate for a respectable royal marriage; he was charming, unscrupulous and feckless – the black sheep of the Teck family. He lived on credit and what he could earn from gambling, and he was conducting a very public liaison with an older married woman. These faults only seemed to encourage Maud's devotion, but her ardour eventually cooled when Prince Frank was packed off to India by his family, out of harm's way and out of reach of his creditors.

Princess Maud's unsuitable affection for Prince Frank at last spurred her mother into action. Queen Victoria, who enjoyed few things more than organising the marriages of her grandchildren, suggested several respectable candidates, among them Prince Max of Baden and her grandson, Prince Ernst Ludwig of Hesse. But Alexandra was determined that no daughter of hers would marry a German. The two sons of her brother, Crown Prince Frederik of Denmark, were both much better suited to marry their English cousin, and Maud eventually settled on the younger and more handsome of the two, Prince Carl.

The wedding took place on 22 July, 1896, in the chapel at Buckingham Palace, with Maud wearing a simple dress of ivory satin, and her mother's wedding veil. They left afterwards for a honeymoon on the Sandringham estate. Five months later they were still there. Maud was twenty-seven years old, but she remained so firmly bound to her mother and the familiar comforts of home that she dreaded leaving England, and delayed her departure for Denmark as long as she could.

'Their Royal Shynesses' Princess Maud (centre) *with her sisters, Victoria and Louise.*

The future Queen of Norway as a child. 'She is a perfect duck and so bewitching,' an aunt said of her. 'I long to squeeze her when I see her.'

But the time eventually came when Prince Carl could no longer postpone his return to the Danish Navy, and Maud was obliged to accompany him across the North Sea just before Christmas 1896.

The new Princess Carl of Denmark received a warm welcome in her new country – she was half-Danish, after all – and soon set about turning her home in the Bernstorf Palace into a replica of Sandringham. She spent her spare time writing long letters to her family, and she went home to England as often as she could. Like all the children of Edward and Alexandra, Maud had been born prematurely and she was dogged by ill-health all her life. The dark Danish winters only exacerbated her neuralgia, bronchitis and migraines.

Princess Maud's only child, Alexander, was born in 1903. By then thirty-three, Maud had hardly changed at all. But then an event took place which forced her to put her childhood behind her at last. Norway had been joined to Sweden for ninety years but, in 1905, it declared itself an independent kingdom and set about finding a monarch of its own. Prince Carl was the final choice, but he would only agree to take the throne if his position was endorsed by Sweden, Denmark and Great Britain, and if the Norwegian people themselves voted their consent in a referendum. The response was overwhelming, and Carl reluctantly accepted the crown in November 1905. He took the traditional Norwegian royal name of Haakon, and Alexander's name was changed to Olav. Maud, a most unwilling queen, refused to change hers.

The coronation of King Haakon and his queen took place at Trondheim in June 1906. It proved an ordeal for Maud, whose aversion to publicity and the public gaze was as strong as ever. But her misgivings were unfounded. 'Charles and Maud did it all in a dignified manner,' May reported afterwards to an aunt, 'and both looked very well with the Crowns on their heads.'

King Haakon proved to be a natural and unassuming monarch, and he soon developed an easy public manner. Maud, though, did not. She never overcame her dislike of the trappings of royalty, and in the company of strangers she often appeared stiff, reserved and cold. Away from the public gaze, though, the Queen was cheerful, warmhearted and amusing, and retained her passion for practical jokes.

(Left) *Princess Maud with her eldest brother, Prince Albert Victor, and* (right) *with Prince Carl of Denmark at the time of their engagement. She and her sister Victoria often dressed alike; see the picture on page 48.*

Queen Maud's only son was christened Alexander but his name was changed to Olav when his father became King of Norway in 1905. He married Princess Märtha of Sweden in 1929 and inherited the throne on his father's death in 1957. King Olav died in 1991, and the crown then passed to his son, Harald.

Norway had no aristocracy and, as the monarchy was so new, no court life either. This suited Haakon and Maud perfectly, as their tastes were simple. All the same, it meant that life was often very lonely for Maud in the vast royal palace in Christiania. It is said that when the queen wanted to dance, a telephone call was made to some young man of good family who would shyly present himself at the palace. The queen would appear and, without saying a word, would dance with him for an hour or two while a major-domo wound the gramophone. Yet the informal, democratic nature of Norwegian life suited Maud well; she was able to go about freely in public in a way that would have been impossible in England, and she became active in championing women's rights and the welfare of unmarried mothers and their children.

Maud continued to visit England regularly, escaping each year from the harsh Norwegian winter to Appleton House, near Sandringham, which her father had given her to be her English home. And it was in London, in November 1938, that she died unexpectedly during a shopping expedition. Haakon was to outlive her by nearly twenty years, and their son, the late King Olav V, who died in 1991, followed their example of selfless, unassuming service to his country.

Prince John 1871

Like all her other children, Princess Alexandra's third son was born prematurely. Because the birth had not been expected so soon, there were no baby clothes and no nurse at Sandringham when her labour began, and the only available medical help was the local doctor.

The child was frail, and when Alexandra awoke in the morning after his birth on 6 April, 1871, she was told that the infant had been christened Alexander John Charles Robert, but had lived only twenty-four hours. Alexandra's unhappiness was only to be expected, but observers were taken aback by the grief of the Prince of Wales. With 'tears rolling down his cheeks', he insisted on placing the child's body in the coffin, and arranging the satin pall and white flowers himself.

The pain of this loss remained with Alexandra for the rest of her life. She was convinced that she alone had been responsible for the death of her son because she had not taken sufficient care during her pregnancy, but others, including Queen Victoria, were inclined to blame the Prince for encouraging his wife to neglect her health. It seems likely, though, that a hormone deficiency in the Princess was the true cause of the premature births of all the Wales children. Although Alexandra was only twenty-six when Prince John died, she was not prepared to risk any further lives. The dead prince was her last child.

The Children of Alice and Ludwig

Victoria
Marchioness of Milford Haven
1863–1950

Elisabeth
Grand Duchess Sergei of Russia
1864–1918

Irene
Princess Heinrich of Prussia
1866–1953

Ernst Ludwig
Grand Duke of Hesse
1868–1937

Friedrich Wilhelm
Prince of Hesse
1870–1873

Alix
Empress Alexandra Feodorovna of Russia
1872–1918

Marie
Princess of Hesse
1874–1878

Alice
& Ludwig of Hesse and by Rhine

The third of Queen Victoria's children was also the first to die. Alice Maud Mary was born in 1843, and once again disappointment was expressed in some quarters at the birth of a daughter. This was not shared by the Queen and Prince Albert, who welcomed the arrival of 'Fat Alice', or 'Fatima', as she was called for a time. Although she was slower to learn than her elder sister, Alice was just as clever, but she was to be overshadowed by Vicky's brilliance all her life. Alice enjoyed a much closer relationship with Bertie than she did with her sister.

In July 1862, Alice was married to Prince Ludwig Karl, heir to the Grand Duke of Hesse and by Rhine. The match had been arranged by Prince Albert, and the ceremony, which took place six months after his death, was a melancholy occasion. Ludwig was a pleasant, straight-forward and kind man, but he lacked Alice's intellectual gifts and their lack of common interests was to cause some tension in their marriage.

Alice found life in Darmstadt very different from the more splendid English court, and she and Ludwig were continually plagued by financial worries and by the fear that Hesse might be absorbed by Prussia. The Princess was much concerned with social problems, and she established societies for the training of nurses and the education of women. Her interest in nursing led to a friendship with Florence Nightingale.

Alice was a carrier of haemophilia and she transmitted the disease to one of her sons and, through her daughters, to three grandsons. The sudden death of her son, Friedrich Wilhelm, was the prelude to a series of tragedies that was to mark the lives of her children. In 1878, her youngest daughter died in a diphtheria epidemic that swept through the entire family, and soon afterwards Alice herself died from the disease, aged thirty-five.

Grand Duke Ludwig's second morganatic marriage in 1884 was annulled on the orders of Queen Victoria, and he died in 1892.

Queen Victoria with her youngest daughter, Princess Beatrice (standing) and her granddaughter, Victoria, Princess Louis of Battenberg. The Princess is holding her eldest daughter, Alice, who later married Prince Andrew of Greece and became the mother of Prince Philip, Duke of Edinburgh.

Victoria,
Marchioness of Milford Haven
1863–1950

When Princess Alice died so suddenly from diphtheria in 1878, her remaining five children were left motherless. They ranged in age from Victoria, who was then fifteen, to Alix, who was six. It was the two youngest, Alix and Ernst Ludwig, who were most deeply affected by their mother's loss, and it was left to Victoria to try and fill the gap. 'My childhood ended with her death,' the princess remembered later, 'for I was the eldest and most responsible of her children.'

But Princess Victoria was not the only one who felt responsible for the young Hessians. Her grandmother, Queen Victoria, had naturally been shocked and distressed by the news, but the fact that her daughter had died on 14 December, the anniversary of the death of the Prince Consort, gave the sad event an almost mystical significance. The Queen wrote in her journal, 'That this dear, talented, distin guished, tender-hearted, noble-minded sweet child . . . should be called back to her father on this very anniversary seems almost incredible, and most mysterious!'

From that time on, the Queen took a particularly tender interest in her grandchildren at Darmstadt. She invited the Grand Duke and the children to come and stay with her at Osborne as soon as possible, and in the years that followed she kept a sharp eye on every detail of the children's lives.

Despite her youth, Princess Victoria was ideally suited to take charge of the family after her mother's death. As a child she had been a tomboy, excelling at climbing trees and on to roofs, and this fearlessness, together with her calm, self-disciplined and practical nature, helped her to keep the family stable and united. In this she was supported by the devoted governess and servants who were more familiar to her than her busy mother had been.

Victoria inherited her mother's radical interests, and she thrived on argument and the support of unorthodox causes. To the end of her life she believed that royalty was anachronistic, although some were to

Princess Victoria of Hesse. She and her younger sisters, Elisabeth and Irene, were known as 'The Three Graces'.

(Right) *Queen Victoria with her son-in-law, Grand Duke Ludwig of Hesse, and his children , in mourning for Princess Alice. From left to right, the children are Princess Victoria, Prince Ernst Ludwig, Princess Irene, Princess Elisabeth and Princess Alix.* (Below) *Princess Victoria and Prince Louis of Battenberg at the time of their engagement in 1883.*

find her aggressive statements of socialist principles somewhat hypocritical, coming as they did from a princess cushioned by wealth and position from the reality of everyday life. She became a confirmed smoker at the age of sixteen, having been introduced to the habit by her cousin, Kaiser Wilhelm II. Queen Victoria heartily disapproved of Victoria's addiction, and the princess was forced to smoke secretly 'up chimneys and out of windows' whenever her grandmother came to stay. Although the princess was to live until she was eighty-seven, her doctors were continually alarmed by her heavy smoking. When one anxious physician urged her to cut her smoking by half, Victoria did exactly that: she cut all her cigarettes in half, without reducing the total number in any way.

In 1884, Victoria was married to Prince Louis of Battenberg. Louis was the eldest son of Prince Alexander of Hesse and his morganatic wife, Countess Julie von Hauke, who had been created Princess of Battenberg. Victoria and Louis had known each other all their lives, although Louis had become a British subject at an early age in order to be able to join the Royal Navy. By the time of his marriage, Prince Louis regarded himself as a British naval officer rather than a German prince.

Victoria's family did not approve of the match. They felt that her first duty should be to her widowed father and younger brother and sisters, and that she should remain at home to care for them. The Prussian and Russian monarchs were also hostile to the marriage, but for rather different reasons: they felt that Louis was not sufficiently royal to marry Victoria, and they disapproved of his British nationality. The ceremony took place, nonetheless, in April 1884, and a vast gathering of European royalty gathered in Darmstadt for the occasion, headed by Queen Victoria.

The married life of Louis and Victoria was calm and harmonious, although they were separated for long periods when the prince was at sea. With the sad exception of their eldest son, George, who died of cancer at the age of forty-six, their four children were to lead long and distinguished lives. Princess Alice married Prince Andrew of Greece and Denmark, and became the mother of Prince Philip, Duke of Edinburgh; Princess Louise married King Gustav VI Adolf of Sweden; and the youngest son, Louis, was created Earl Mountbatten of Burma.

The charm and ability of Prince Louis had won him rapid advancement in the Royal Navy but, on the outbreak of the First World War, he was forced to resign as First Sea Lord. Despite his British nationality and his fierce loyalty to the country of his adoption, a public outcry against all things German made his position intolerable. In 1917, King George V abolished all German titles in the British royal family, and Louis and Victoria took the surname Mountbatten and became the first Marquess and Marchioness of Milford Haven. Victoria was not pleased by the change, saying that she would rather have no title at all than join the ranks of 'brewers, lawyers and bankers Peers'.

The end of the war was to bring the first of the many tragedies that were to punctuate Victoria's remaining years. The deaths of her younger sisters, Alix, Empress of Russia, and Elisabeth, the Grand Duchess Sergei, in the Russian Revolution; the sudden death from a heart attack of Prince Louis in 1921; the lingering death of her son, George, in 1938; the loss of her nephew and his wife and sons in a plane crash at Ostend in 1937 – these misfortunes were to test Victoria's endurance to the full. Princess Victoria died at Kensington Palace in 1950, having had the satisfaction of seeing her grandson married to the future Queen Elizabeth II.

(Above) *Princess Victoria in 1905 with her daughter, Alice, and her first grandchild, Princess Margarita.* (Below) *Victoria, Dowager Marchioness of Milford Haven, shortly before the Second World War.*

A family group at Coburg in April 1894 at the time of the wedding of Grand Duke Ernst Ludwig of Hesse and Princess Victoria Melita of Edinburgh. (Standing left to right) *Tsarevitch Nicholas of Russia, Princess Alix of Hesse, Victoria, Princess Louis of Battenberg, Grand Duke Ernst Ludwig.* (Seated, left to right) *Irene, Princess Heinrich of Prussia, Elisabeth, Grand Duchess Sergei of Russia, Grand Duchess Victoria Melita, Grand Duke Sergei of Russia.*

Elisabeth,
Grand Duchess Sergei of Russia
1864–1918

Princess Alice's second child, Elisabeth, was the only member of her family to escape the tragic diphtheria epidemic of 1878. When the first of her sisters became ill, Elisabeth – known to her family as Ella – was sent to stay with her paternal grandmother, Princess Karl of Hesse, and so was spared the suffering that was to cost the lives of her mother and youngest sister. Ella was just one year younger than Victoria and, after the death of Princess Alice, shared with her the responsibility of caring for the Grand Duke and their brother and sisters. In a way this was a blessing in disguise, for it helped the young princesses to forget their own unhappiness. Even at this early age, though, it seemed that the relief of the pain and suffering of others was to be Ella's prime concern. 'It has been said that death is a dark lattice that lets in a bright day,' the fourteen year old princess wrote to her grieving grand mother, Queen Victoria, 'and may that comfort you.'

Apart from her tender concern for the welfare of others, Ella's most noteworthy characteristic was her breathtaking beauty, and suitors flocked round her as she grew older. One of the most persistent of these was her cousin, the future Kaiser Wilhelm II, who decided that Ella was to be his wife. He did not take kindly to her firm refusal of his proposal, and for many years afterwards he spread rumours about her marriage, and went out of his way to avoid meeting her.

At the time of Wilhelm's unwelcome proposal, Ella had already set her heart on marrying the Grand Duke Sergei Alexandrovitch, fifth son of Tsar Alexander II of Russia. Their engagement was announced in 1884, shortly before her sister Victoria's marriage to Prince Louis of Battenberg. Sergei and Ella had known each other all their lives, for his mother, the Empress Marie, had been born a princess of Hesse, and the young Sergei had spent many childhood holidays with his cousins in Darmstadt. Ella and Sergei were devoted to one another, but her family was not altogether happy about their marriage. Sergei was certainly handsome and imposing, but he had an austere, reserved

Princess Elisabeth (standing) *with her sister, Victoria* (left) *and her aunt, Princess Beatrice.*

(Above) *Elisabeth and Sergei dressed for a costume ball in the early years of their marriage* (Below) *The Grand Duke and Grand Duchess Sergei at home.*

manner that made him appear cruel and somewhat frightening.

The wedding of Ella and Sergei took place in St Petersburg in June 1888. After the lengthy and magnificent marriage ceremonies, they spent a quiet honeymoon in the country, where Ella encountered for the first time the servility and destitution of the Russian peasantry. The early years of her married life were happy and splendid. Sergei adored her, and she soon became a brilliant hostess and leader of fashion, taking great pleasure in jewels, clothes and the glittering life of the Court and Society. Ella's beauty became legendary, and her cousin, Queen Marie of Romania, remembered her at this time as being 'so fairy-like an apparition that I would like to dip my pen in colour, so as to be able to make her live again, if only for a moment, because eyes that have never beheld her will never be able to conceive what she was.'

Soon after a visit with Sergei to the Holy Land, Ella decided to change her religion to Russian Orthodox. There was no requirement for her to do this, as Sergei was not in line for the throne, but she was devoted to her husband and wanted to identify herself more closely with her adopted country and its people. The news of Ella's conversion was not well received by her family, who suspected that Sergei had forced her to take this step.

By the late 1890s, there was increasing unrest in Russia among students and malcontents, and their protests were being met with arrests and deportations. In 1891, Sergei was appointed Governor-General of Moscow and became the focus for much of this discontent. He countered it with the implementation of increasingly violent and repressive measures but these seemed to have little effect. And then, on 17 February, 1905, Sergei was blown to pieces by a bomb.

Ella reacted to Sergei's death with astonishing self-control. Two days later she went to the prison where the assassin was being held to ask him to repent for killing her husband. The man, a student named Kaliaev, told her that he had acted according to his principles and regretted nothing. Ella promised to pray for him, and told him that she would care for his mother for as long as she lived.

In the weeks that followed, Ella began a slow withdrawal from the world. She stopped eating meat, stripped her apartments of their rich furnishings, and gave away her fashionable clothes. She disposed of her jewels, too, returning heirlooms to the Tsar and giving others to relatives. From that time on she wore a plain nun's habit, and declared that she would now devote her life to the relief of poverty and suffering.

In 1910, Ella founded the Order of Martha and Mary, the only sisterhood of nursing nuns in Russia. She built a large hospital, which included an orphanage and old people's home, and spent her time in active philanthropy in the worst Moscow slums. She did not cut herself off entirely from the Imperial family; she attended weddings and private family celebrations but she never went to balls or other entertainments. There were rumours that Ella's asceticism was a pose and that she lived a secret life of luxury behind the walls of her convent, but nothing could have been further from the truth. The poor of Moscow were well aware of her genuine, active concern for their welfare.

The Grand Duchess Sergei in her nun's habit. She became known as 'Little Mother' to the poor of Moscow.

Ella made a point of never interfering in politics but she broke this rule when she tried to warn the Tsar about the malign influence of Rasputin. The Empress, Ella's sister, refused to allow her to see her husband and refused, too, to listen to any criticism of Rasputin. Despite this rebuff, Ella continued to work throughout the First World War, enduring increasing vilification because of her German origins. Kaiser Wilhelm himself, remembering his past love for her, pleaded with Ella to leave Russia before it was too late but she refused to abandon her work or desert her sister, the Empress. Neither the abdication of the Tsar in 1917 nor the coming to power of the Bolshevik government could distract Ella from her work among the poor and needy.

In the spring of 1918 Ella was arrested. Accompanied only by her companion, Sister Barbara, she was taken across Russia to Siberia, where she was imprisoned with five Romanov Grand Dukes in a former school in the town of Alpaevsk. In July, the prisoners were herded into a lorry and driven into a forest. They were taken to a disused mine shaft and, one by one, pushed over the edge. The soldiers flung two hand grenades into the shaft after them.

A little time afterwards a monk called Father Seraphim climbed down the shaft and retrieved the bodies of Ella and Sister Barbara. He vowed that he would take them to the Holy Land for burial and for two years he struggled with the coffins across Russia and into China. In 1920, Ella's sister, Victoria, by then Marchioness of Milford Haven, heard that the bodies were enshrined in a Russian Orthodox chapel in Peking and arranged for them to be taken to Jerusalem. In April 1921, she and Prince Louis, together with the devoted Father Seraphim, were present when Ella was laid to rest at last in the Russian Orthodox church on the Mount of Olives.

Irene, Princess Heinrich of Prussia
1866–1953

Princess Irene after her marriage to another of Queen Victoria's grandchildren, Prince Heinrich of Prussia.

Princess Irene, the third child of Princess Alice and Grand Duke Ludwig, was born in 1866, nearly two years after her sister, Ella. Her christening took place on the day that the Austro-Prussian war was formally ended, and because of this she was named 'Irene', a derivation of the Greek word for 'peace'.

A family friend once described the eldest daughters of Princess Alice as 'The Three Graces', and Irene certainly shared the charm and beauty of her sisters. Unlike the others, though, her life was calm, happy and undisturbed by scandal or dissension. In 1888, she married her first cousin, Prince Heinrich of Prussia and they enjoyed a long and harmonious life together. 'The Very Amiables', as they were known in the family, were popular with all their relations.

Despite her calm, well-ordered life, Princess Irene endured two great tragedies. She, like her mother, was a carrier of haemophilia, and she passed this disease to two of her three sons. The youngest, Heinrich, died of haemophilia at the age of four, but Waldemar survived until 1945. Irene's second son, Sigismund, did not suffer from haemophilia. He left Germany in 1922 to grow coffee in Guatemala, and died in Costa Rica in 1979. The second great sorrow of Irene's life came with the outbreak of the First World War, when she found herself on the opposing side to her sisters, Victoria, Ella and Alix. It was primarily because of his relationship to Irene, whose husband was in command of the German fleet, that Prince Louis of Battenberg was forced to resign as First Sea Lord.

In 1922, Princess Irene was drawn into the dispute over the identity of the mysterious 'Anna Anderson' who claimed to be the Grand Duchess Anastasia, youngest daughter of the murdered Tsar Nicholas II. Irene visited the claimant in hospital and announced afterwards that she could not possibly be her niece. Shortly before her death, however, she admitted to a friend that she 'might have made a mistake and that it probably was Anastasia'.

Ernst Ludwig, Grand Duke of Hesse
1868–1937

When Prince Ernst Ludwig was five years old, he saw his younger brother Friedrich Wilhelm, nicknamed Frittie, fall to his death from a window of his mother's bedroom. The prince was deeply shocked by this event, and it was to haunt him for the rest of his life. Ernie, as he was known in the family, had always been a sensitive child, tortured by a fear of death. When he was three, he had told his nurse that he didn't want her to die alone. 'We must all die together,' he had sobbed. Later, after the death of his brother, he repeated this fear to his mother. 'When I die, you must die too,' he told her. 'I don't want to die alone, like Frittie.'

In 1878, when Ernie was ten years old, the Grand Ducal family was struck down by an epidemic of diphtheria. The Grand Duke and all the children, with the exception of the absent Ella, caught the disease, and on 16 November the youngest daughter, May, died. The news of the death of his favourite sister was kept from Ernie, who was himself seriously ill. But he kept asking to see her, and sent messages to her, and in the end Princess Alice could no longer keep the news from him. Overcome with love and sympathy for her grieving son, Alice put her arms around him and kissed him. This kiss was enough to pass the disease to her, and she died on 14 December, four weeks after the death of her daughter.

Ernie never recovered from this second shock, and he would always blame himself for having caused his mother's death. He grew to maturity pampered and spoiled by his sisters, and developed a deep interest in poetry, painting and music, as well as a fondness for interior decoration and arranging flowers. He had inherited his mother's intelligence and her interest in literature and art, and he studied at the universities of Leipzig and Giessen. He abandoned a career in the army when his father died.

In 1892, at the age of twenty-three, Ernie became Grand Duke of Hesse. It was then that his grandmother, Queen Victoria, decided that

Prince Ernst Ludwig was twenty-three when he became Grand Duke of Hesse on his father's death. Although he was unprepared to govern, he was able to abandon his military career and pursue his artistic interests.

Prince Ernst Ludwig in 1876 with his three youngest sisters, Irene, Alix and Marie.

he should marry his first cousin, Princess Victoria Melita of Edinburgh. Ernie and Ducky, as she was called, had known each other all their lives and they had a great deal in common. They shared an interest in art and enjoyed practical jokes; they had the same sense of humour and adored music, amateur theatricals and arranging flowers.

With the marriage of Ernie and Ducky, life at the Hessian court in Darmstadt assumed a new vitality. The Grand Duke and his new Duchess pursued a life of hectic enjoyment, and Prince Nicholas of Greece remembered one weekend at Darmstadt as being 'the jolliest, merriest house party I have ever been to in my life.' Tennis, riding, picnics, private theatricals, excursions to the races, jousting on bicycles – there seemed no end to the entertainment they provided for their guests. The only interest which Ernie and Ducky did not share was riding – she had a collection of white Lippizaner horses as well as a black stallion called Bogdan who would obey no one else. Ernie was once seen flying up the steps of the palace, screaming with fear, with this stallion in hot pursuit. Ducky, for her part, could not understand Ernie's lack of interest in horses or his frequent objections to her disappearing for hours on end on long rides.

In 1895 their only child, Elisabeth, was born, and soon after that it became clear that the marriage of Ernie and Ducky was a failure. There were violent arguments and much throwing of crockery. Ducky neglected her official duties and objected when Ernie complained. The rowdy house parties continued but guests now noticed the strain and tension in their relationship. The cause of the disenchantment was simple: Ducky had fallen in love with another cousin, Grand Duke Kirill of Russia, while Ernie's tastes lay in quite a different direction. 'No boy was safe,' Ducky is said to have told a niece later. 'From the stable hands to the kitchen help, he slept quite openly with them all.' Both Ernie and Ducky wished to end their marriage but this was impossible while their grandmother lived. 'I arranged that marriage,' Queen Victoria said. 'I will never try and marry anyone again.' The Queen would not countenance either separation or a divorce, and they had to wait until her death in 1901 before they were, at last, able to end their marriage.

The divorce caused a scandal, and it was not until 1905 that Ernie and Ducky were free to marry again. Their daughter Elisabeth had died suddenly of typhoid in 1903, and so Ernie was left alone in the palace at Darmstadt. He then decided to marry again, if only to secure the succession to the Grand Duchy. His new bride, Princess Eleonore of Solms-Hohensolms-Lich, may have lacked Ducky's beauty and temperament but she was far better suited to the life of a Grand Duchess. She performed all the ceremonial duties that Ducky had neglected, appeared to be a devoted wife, and gave Ernie two sons, Georg and Ludwig.

Ernie's life was peaceful at last, and in the years preceding the First World War he was able to indulge his artistic interests to the full, organising festivals of music and art at Darmstadt, and establishing the reputation of the Court Theatre and orchestra. When the war came, he refused to join the Kaiser's armies, and devoted his energies instead to the care of the wounded and to visiting hospitals. When hostilities ceased, he turned his attention to the mental and physical rehabilitation of young casualties of the war. In 1918, Hesse became a republic and Ernie abdicated, although he continued to live in some state in his home, Schloss Wolfsgarten, until his death.

Ernst Ludwig with the infant Hereditary Grand Duke Georg, his eldest son by his second marriage to Princess Eleonore of Solms-Hohensolms-Lich. In November 1937, Georg and his mother, wife and two sons were all killed in an air crash near Ostend.

Prince Friedrich Wilhelm of Hesse
1870–1873

Prince Friedrich Wilhelm's eldest sister, Victoria, called him 'a very pretty winsome child', and he was the apple of his mother's eye.

Three of Princess Alice's children were to be affected in different ways by haemophilia. Irene and Alix passed the disease to their sons, but it was Prince Friedrich Wilhelm, known in the family as Frittie, who was to suffer directly from it.

Frittie was born on 7 October, 1870, and this playful, bright and charming prince soon became the apple of his mother's eye. His health gave rise to some concern from the first, but it was not until February 1873, when the prince bled for three days after cutting an ear, that it was confirmed that he was suffering from haemophilia. Even then there seemed no immediate cause for alarm, although it was now necessary to exercise increased caution and vigilance. And then, in May of that year, while playing in his mother's bedroom with his brother, Ernie, the young prince climbed on to a chair to peer out of a window and fell on to the balcony below. The fall was not a particularly serious one and the prince had no visible injuries, but he never recovered consciousness, and died shortly afterwards from internal bleeding to the brain.

Princess Alice never recovered from the death of her adored son. 'He seems near me always,' she wrote to Queen Victoria later, 'and I carry his precious image in my heart everywhere. That can never fade or die!'

Of all the expressions of sympathy that Alice received after Frittie's death, perhaps the most poignant was to come from her brother, Prince Leopold, who was the only one of Queen Victoria's sons to suffer from haemophilia. 'I know too well what it is to suffer as he would have suffered,' the prince wrote, 'and the great trials of not being able to enjoy life or to know what happiness is, like others . . . I cannot help saying to myself that it is perhaps well that the dear child has been spared all the trials and possibly miseries of a life of ill health like mine.'

Alix,
Empress Alexandra Feodorovna of Russia 1872–1918

Princess Alice had hoped to give her fourth daughter her own name but the Germans found it difficult to pronounce and so the child was called Alix instead. The young princess was sweet-natured, cheerful and mischievous, and her nickname, Sunny, seemed to suit her perfectly. But all this changed when her mother died. The happy, laughing princess became silent and withdrawn, keeping herself aloof from strangers and presenting an unsmiling, melancholy face to the world.

Alix's beauty attracted much attention as she grew older, but it was when she attended her sister Ella's wedding in St Petersburg that she first caught the eye of the heir to the Russian throne. The Tsarevitch Nicholas was then only sixteen and Alix was twelve but he was charmed by her, and gave her a brooch which so flustered her that she immediately gave it back. Alix was as enchanted by Nicholas as he was by her, and their friendship developed into love. But Nicholas was not the only royal heir to be attracted by Alix. Prince Albert Victor, eldest son of the Prince of Wales, also fell in love with his beautiful Hessian cousin. Queen Victoria heartily approved the idea of a match between these two grandchildren but few shared her opinion, least of all Princess Alix herself.

In 1894, the Tsarevitch Nicholas came to Darmstadt to attend the wedding of Alix's brother, Ernie, and he proposed to her on the morning of his arrival. At first Alix refused: she was deeply religious, and would not contemplate changing her religion from Protestant to Russian Orthodox. But Nicholas was insistent and, the day after the wedding, Alix at last accepted, encouraged by the example of her sister Ella, who had herself converted to the Russian Orthodox faith after her marriage to Grand Duke Sergei.

There was no doubt at all about the intense love that Alix and Nicholas felt for one another. 'You are locked in my heart,' Alix wrote to him soon after their engagement. 'The little key is lost and now you must stay there forever.' To many, though, their marriage seemed

Queen Victoria found it hard to believe that 'gentle, simple Alicky should be the great Empress of Russia.'

(Above) *Princess Alix* (seated) *preparing for her first ball in 1889, helped by her sister, Elisabeth, and Mrs Orchard, their English nurse.* (Above right) *Tsar Nicholas and the Empress Alexandra at the Romanov tercentenary celebrations in 1913.*

(Opposite) *Empress Alexandra* (seated left) *with her first child, the Grand Duchess Olga, on a visit to Queen Victoria at Balmoral in 1896. Standing behind are Tsar Nicholas and the Prince of Wales, later King Edward VII.*

likely to be a union of opposites. Alix was statuesque, dignified and clever, possessed of a strong will and iron determination. Nicholas, on the other hand, was soft-hearted, generous and devoted, but he lacked confidence and self-assurance and he was completely dominated by his intimidating parents and a battery of formidable uncles. He looked to Alix to protect him from his parents and to support him when he became Tsar, while she was attracted by his charm and helplessness. They were both completely unsuited to the parts they would have to play in the drama that lay ahead.

Tsar Alexander died at the beginning of November, 1894, and the nervous twenty-six year-old Nicholas became the absolute monarch of Russia. At the end of the month, he and Alix were married in St Petersburg. On her conversion, she had changed her name; Princess Alix of Hesse and by Rhine was now Alexandra Feodorovna, Empress of All the Russias.

From the first, Nicholas and Alix were supremely happy together. 'I would never have believed that one could have so perfect a happiness in this world,' she wrote to him on the morning after their wedding, but the happiness of their married life was not echoed in their relationship

Nicholas was twenty-six when he became Tsar, and Alix was twenty-two. Their first child, Grand Duchess Olga (below) was born a year later in 1895. Queen Victoria thought the baby 'magnificent . . . a lovely, lively great-grandchild.'

with the rest of the Imperial family, or with the country at large. Nicholas's mother, the Dowager Empress Marie Feodorovna, refused to relinquish the powers and privilege she had enjoyed, and insisted on taking precedence over her daughter-in-law. She treated Nicholas like a little boy. He was dominated, too, by his overbearing uncles, but the abilities of the new Tsar were, in any case, severely limited. He seemed unable to follow the advice of others and he made unwise ministerial appointments, tried to avoid making difficult decisions, and tended to agree with every suggestion he was offered. Alix, on the other hand, behaved exactly as an Empress should. She looked magnificent in her elaborate robes and jewels, and her dignified bearing suited the part admirably. But she was shy and nervous on public occasions, and this made her seem hard and aloof. She never smiled in public or appeared to enjoy herself, and she seemed unwilling or unable to make the slightest spontaneous gesture.

In the country at large, Imperial rule was slowly crumbling as Nicholas resisted increasing demands for more democratic government and relief of the poverty and hardship endured by the vast majority of the population. He could not or would not comprehend the principles of parliamentary government, and Alix supported him in his resistance to any change. From the beginning, his reign was punctuated by unrest. Riots, attempted assassinations, unofficial strikes and anti-Jewish pogroms all contributed to the growing instability of the country, as did the humiliating defeat of the Russian fleet in the war with Japan in 1904–5. Nicholas then gave in to popular demand and assigned some powers to a new parliament, the *Duma*, but he promptly dissolved this assembly two years later.

By now the calm domestic life of Alix and Nicholas had been shattered by the discovery that their only son, Alexei, was haemophiliac. Between 1895 and 1901, four daughters – Olga, Tatiana, Maria and Anastasia – were born to the Imperial couple. Alix and Nicholas adored these lively and attractive children, but their particular hope was for a son to inherit the throne, and so, when Alexei was born in 1904, their happiness seemed complete. From the first, though, this happiness was tinged with anxiety about the child's health, and their worst fears were confirmed six weeks after his birth, when he bled from the navel for three days. Alexei's parents were distraught for there was then no known treatment and no cure for haemophilia. All they could do was make sure that Alexei avoided all injury, and two sailors were assigned to stay by his side every minute of the day. Above all, his illness had to be kept secret.

Alix was consumed with guilt, knowing that she had transmitted the disease to her son, and this knowledge, combined with grief and despair at her child's acute suffering, only made her more withdrawn and neurotic. Had she inherited more of her mother's keen intellect and commonsense, she might have been better able to cope with the demands of the situation but, as it was, her vulnerable and credulous nature made her easily susceptible to the hypnotic persuasiveness of Rasputin.

Grigoriy Rasputin was a Siberian peasant mystic possessed of apparently extraordinary powers. Holy men of this kind had always been common in Russia and were often taken up by fashionable society, as Rasputin was. He was introduced to the Imperial couple in 1905, and they became convinced that he was a genuine 'man of God' when he restored Alexei to full health after a particularly severe period of pain. From that time on, as Rasputin again and again relieved the boy's agony when others could not, the monk became indispensable to Alix and Nicholas. Alix especially was convinced that Rasputin had miraculous healing powers, and he was allowed unprecedented freedom of speech and conduct in her presence. In Alix's eyes, Rasputin was not just a miraculous healer; he seemed to personify the loyal, devout, unchanging Russia of her imagination.

Rasputin's hold over the Imperial family now seems completely inexplicable but, at the time, he came to assume unparalleled influence over the Tsar and his wife. Decisions were made and government ministers dismissed on his advice, and Alix and Nicholas refused to tolerate any criticism of him. They would not listen to accounts of his sexual excesses and his insolence to others; to them, this evil-smelling, unwashed, arrogant, ambitious peasant could do no wrong. But, as Rasputin's influence grew, so did antagonism towards him. He was rumoured to be Alix's lover and, when the First World War broke out, it was said that he and Alix were working together to secure a German victory. But Nicholas and Alix still would not listen to reason, and so, at the end of 1916, a group of aristocrats took the law into their own hands and murdered Rasputin in St Petersburg. Alix was horrified by Rasputin's death. He had once told her that if he died, then she would lose her son and her crown within six months. In this instance Rasputin had been mistaken: it took three months, not six.

In March 1917, there were riots in St Petersburg followed by a mutiny of troops. Law and order collapsed, and a reconvened *Duma* declared a new provisional government, headed by Alexander Kerensky. The army defected to the revolutionaries and, on 15

The hypnotic powers of the Siberian monk, Rasputin (above), *enabled him to exercise extraordinary influence over the Empress, who is seen* (below) *with the Tsar and their son, the haemophiliac Tsarevitch Alexei*

(Above) *Nicholas and Alexandra with the infant Tsarevitch Alexei and their four daughters, Tatiana, Marie, Anastasia and Olga.* (Right) *The Tsar with the Tsarevitch Alexei and his second daughter, Grand Duchess Tatiana, in 1916.*

March, Nicholas abdicated. He was imprisoned with his family, first at the palace of Tsarskoe Seloe, and then at Tobolsk in Siberia. In November 1917, Kerensky's government was overthrown, and Lenin and the Bolsheviks came to power. The Imperial family were then moved to Ekaterinburg, near the Ural mountains, and it was there, on the night of 16 July, 1918, that Alix and Nicholas, together with Alexei and their four daughters, were murdered.

The actual events of that night are still uncertain. Despite the absence of clear evidence, it has always been assumed that the entire family died together in a cellar in the 'House of Special Purpose' at Ekaterinburg. But there is convincing evidence to suggest that only the Tsar and his son were killed that night, and that Alix and her daughters were moved elsewhere and were still alive some months later. It has also been convincingly suggested that the youngest daughter, the Grand Duchess Anastasia, escaped and found her way to Berlin in 1920. The mysterious 'Anna Anderson' may have failed in her attempt to prove beyond doubt that she was Anastasia, but her opponents also failed to prove that she was someone else. 'Anna Anderson' died in 1984, but the mystery of her identity remains unsolved.

Princess Marie of Hesse

1874–1878

Marie, the seventh and last child of Princess Alice, was born on 24 May, 1874, almost exactly a year after the death of her brother, Frittie. The young princess, nicknamed May, was adored by Alix and Ernie, and their mother lavished particular affection on her three younger children.

On 6 November, 1878, first Victoria and then Alix fell ill with diphtheria, to be followed by May, Irene, Ernie and then their father, the Grand Duke Ludwig. Princess Alice personally took charge of the nursing arrangements, but she still found time to send reports to Queen Victoria. On 15 November she wrote: 'And my sweet little May *so bad* – so bad; will she get through it! My little one – my last! Oh, it is agony!' The next day a telegram arrived at Balmoral to tell the Queen that the little princess had died.

The news of May's death had to be kept from the other children, and so the grief of Princess Alice was intensified by the need to behave as though nothing had happened and to conduct May's funeral without them knowing. It was not until the beginning of December that Alice could bring herself to break the news to Ernie, and it was her spontaneous, comforting embrace that resulted in her catching the infection herself. She died on 14 December, four weeks after the death of her 'sweet May'.

Princess Marie photographed at Eastbourne in the summer of 1878 when Princess Alice and her family spent a holiday there as guests of Queen Victoria.

The Children of Alfred and Marie

Alfred
Hereditary Prince of Saxe-Coburg and Gotha
1874–1899

Marie
Queen of Romania
1875–1938

Victoria Melita
Grand Duchess Kirill of Russia
1876–1936

Alexandra
Princess of Hohenlohe-Langenburg
1878–1942

Beatrice
Infanta of Spain
1884–1966

Alfred
& Marie of Russia

With the birth of Prince Alfred in 1844, Queen Victoria and Prince Albert now had four children, all under the age of four. The future of their second son was decided at an early age: he would inherit the Dukedom of Saxe-Coburg and Gotha in the likely event of the reigning Duke, who was Albert's brother, dying without an heir. Affie, as he was known, was a clever, charming and quick-witted child, and from infancy he displayed a fascination with ships and the sea. It was therefore inevitable that he would make a career in the Navy before coming into his Coburg inheritance.

Affie joined the Royal Navy in 1858 and from then on spent much of his time away from England, becoming the least known and least popular of Queen Victoria's sons. In 1862 he was offered the throne of Greece, which he declined because of his commitment to Coburg and the Navy. He was created Duke of Edinburgh in 1866, and in 1873 he became engaged to Grand Duchess Marie of Russia, the only daughter of Tsar Alexander II. This match was unpopular in England and in Russia but Alfred persisted, perhaps because the plump, plain Marie was reputed to be the richest princess in Europe. She was also said to be the most unpopular princess, a reputation confirmed by her subsequent behaviour in England, where her arrogant attitudes and violent dislike of English food, weather and society won her few friends.

In 1893, at the age of fifty, Affie inherited the Dukedom of Saxe-Coburg and he and his wife took up permanent residence there. Marie enjoyed being the consort of a reigning prince, but Affie regretted leaving the Navy. He became an increasingly heavy drinker and his marriage, which had never been happy, suffered in consequence. In 1900, Affie died of cancer of the throat, the third of Queen Victoria's children to predecease her. Duchess Marie lived on until 1920, when she died in Zurich.

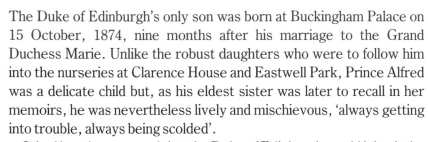

Alfred, Hereditary Prince of Saxe-Coburg and Gotha 1874–1899

Prince Alfred in 1890, photographed in his Prussian Guards uniform.

The Duke of Edinburgh's only son was born at Buckingham Palace on 15 October, 1874, nine months after his marriage to the Grand Duchess Marie. Unlike the robust daughters who were to follow him into the nurseries at Clarence House and Eastwell Park, Prince Alfred was a delicate child but, as his eldest sister was later to recall in her memoirs, he was nevertheless lively and mischievous, 'always getting into trouble, always being scolded'.

It had long been agreed that the Duke of Edinburgh would inherit the dukedom of Saxe-Coburg and Gotha on the death of his childless uncle, Duke Ernst II, and he now decided to educate his own son, Prince Alfred, in Germany, to better prepare him for his eventual succession and for his future life as a German ruling prince. So in 1883, nine year-old Alfred was sent to live alone in Coburg, where he was placed in the care of Dr Wilhelm Rolfs, a self-opinionated but clever disciplinarian who was much admired by the Duchess of Edinburgh. Alfred's sister, Marie, was later to describe Rolfs as an example of 'German *Kultur* at its worst, arrogant, masterful, over-ruling everyone else, turning the best into ridicule, laying down the law, intolerant, tyrannical.' He was also a fervent Anglophobe and took pleasure in ridiculing his pupil in front of others. Alfred's solitary life in Coburg was miserable enough without the additional burden of Rolf's insensitivity, and this cruel early separation from his family was to leave an indelible mark on the prince's emotional development.

In 1889, the Duke of Edinburgh and the rest of his family joined Alfred in Coburg, and Rolfs was appointed to educate his sisters as well. Unlike his wife, the Duke loathed Rolfs and did his best to have him removed, but it was not until four years later that the tutor was eventually dismissed. By this time, Prince Alfred had moved to Potsdam where he was serving with the 1st Regiment of Prussian Guards. From then on he saw little of his family, and began to lead an increasingly dissipated life.

By 1896, Prince Alfred was suffering from venereal disease and had been discharged from his regiment. His mother, Duchess Marie, was appalled at what had happened. Neither she nor his often absent father were ever able to give Alfred the sympathy and support he so desperately needed. Now, disgusted and embarrassed by her son's illness, the Duchess sent him to stay with her eldest daughter, Marie, then Crown Princess of Romania, in the hope that she might persuade Alfred to mend his ways. Marie's attempts to reform her brother failed, and when she arrived in Gotha in the spring of 1899 to attend her parents' silver wedding celebrations, she found that his condition had gravely deteriorated. 'He hardly recognises anyone,' Marie wrote to one of her sisters, 'and often does not know what he says, poor boy.' Shortly afterwards, at the height of the celebrations, Prince Alfred shot himself.

The wound was not fatal, but the prince was severely injured. Even so, his angry and embarrassed mother ignored the advice of doctors and insisted that Alfred be moved immediately to Merano in Switzerland. But the journey proved too much for him, and the prince died on 6 February, 1899, quite alone except for a doctor and a manservant.

Prince Alfred's family were shocked and distressed by his death, but their immediate reaction was to conceal the true cause. *The Times* reported that the prince had died of 'a tumour'. Other versions merely stated that Alfred's health had 'broken down', or else ascribed the cause of death to consumption. Even his closest relations seemed uncertain of the true circumstances, apart from the fact that the prince had died as a result of the dissipated life he had led in Berlin.

Despite the sadness and uncertainty surrounding his early death, Prince Alfred was remembered by many with affection. 'I loved that boy,' his aunt, the Empress Friedrich, wrote to a daughter. 'There was something irresistibly taking about him. He was one of those who are not fit to take care of themselves, not from evil disposition but from weakness of character.'

(Above) *Prince Alfred, aged six, with his sister Marie.* (Below) *Alfred, aged sixteen, with his father the Duke of Edinburgh* (right) *and his cousins, Prince Ernst Ludwig of Hesse* (left) *and Prince George of Wales.*

Princess Marie, aged ten (top left) *and fifteen* (top right). *She is seen* (bottom left) *with Princess Marie, in 1902, and* (far right) *at the time of her engagement to Crown Prince Ferdinand of Romania.*

Marie, Queen of Romania
1875–1938

Of all Queen Victoria's grandchildren, Marie of Romania was perhaps the most extraordinary. Vain, radiant, beautiful, absurd, outrageous, and courageous – she became a legend in her own lifetime, thanks to her undoubted gifts and to a remarkable talent for self-publicity. Modesty, though, was never her strongest point. She once wrote, 'I am said to be the most beautiful woman in Europe. About that, of course, I cannot judge because I cannot know. But about the other queens, I know. I am the most beautiful queen in Europe.' Contemporary verdicts only confirm Queen Marie's high opinion of herself. One royal observer noted that Marie was 'the most beautiful woman I ever saw' and it has also been written of her that 'she formed a whole generation – every man was in love with her, every artist inspired by her, every woman wished to look like her.'

Marie – or Missy, as she was always known to her relations – was born on 29 October, 1875 at Eastwell Park in Kent, the country home of the Duke of Edinburgh.

Princess Marie and her sisters inherited from their mother a fascination with the splendours of the East and a very high opinion of themselves. 'I grew up an exceedingly royal little person,' Queen Marie later wrote, 'full of my own importance, and in the belief that our glory, like that of the sun, was an unquestioned reality.' And so it was not surprising that when the Prince of Wales's second son, George, asked for Marie's hand in marriage, she had no hesitation in turning him down. Her mother encouraged this refusal; she had no intention of allowing any of her daughters to marry an English prince. Had she known that George would become heir to the throne on the death of his elder brother, Prince Albert Victor, the Duchess might well have changed her mind but, as things stood, she had another royal suitor in mind for her daughter.

One of Marie's aunts described Crown Prince Ferdinand of Romania as 'unprepossessing', and this shy, tongue-tied prince was certainly a

Queen Marie leaving the Ritz-Carlton Hotel, New York, after a Grand Ball given in her honour during her American tour in 1926.

(Right) *Queen Marie in the uniform of the Romanian Cavalry.*

During the First World War, Marie spent much of her time visiting wounded soldiers in hospital. The photograph of the Queen in Red Cross uniform was taken to give away to her admiring subjects.

far less personable candidate than George of Wales. But one day Ferdinand would reign in Romania, and this was his chief virtue in the eyes of the Duchess. When he and Marie became engaged in 1892, the announcement was greeted with anger by the Prince of Wales, who felt that his son had been snubbed, and with alarm by Queen Victoria. Nevertheless, the marriage took place early in 1893, and seventeen-year-old Marie, bewildered, anxious and homesick, arrived in Bucharest as the new Crown Princess of Romania. 'I must have looked exactly what I was,' Marie remembered later, 'an innocent little fool with a head stuffed full of illusions and dreams.'

In the years that followed, Marie was to indulge her illusions and dreams to the full, but the early months of her marriage were miserable. Her young husband was withdrawn and diffident, unable to offer her the companionship she craved. King Carol was distant and intimidating, and the Queen – the extraordinary poet-queen, Carmen Sylva – had been banished from court. But, as Marie became accustomed to her new position, she began to assert her authority. She rebelled against the tyrannical King as much as she was able, and became extremely popular in the country by giving birth to an heir, Prince Carol, and by displaying an increasing fascination with the landscape and traditions of Romania.

Marie was to have two further sons and three daughters, but the arrival of her children did little to dim her vitality, and, as she grew older, she began to gain a reputation for frivolity, flirtatiousness, wilfulness and theatricality. Her beauty became legendary. 'I have seldom seen so lovely a creature,' wrote her aunt, the Empress Friedrich of Germany. 'She is a perfect picture.' Marie was not one to allow her beauty to go unnoticed. She dressed as flamboyantly as possible in diaphanous embroidered gowns, cloaks and trailing draperies, and was photographed as often as she could manage in the part-Byzantine, part-Art Nouveau splendour of her palace at Cotroceni, often in Hussar uniform or Romanian national costume.

Shortly after the start of the First World War, King Carol died and Marie became queen at last. 'At that hour I knew that I had won, that the stranger, the girl who had come from over the seas, was a stranger no more; I was theirs with every drop of my blood!'

During the war, Queen Marie became a focus for Romanian nationalism and she worked tirelessly in Red Cross hospitals, romantically garbed in nurse's uniform. And, when hostilities ceased, she resumed her regal rôle. 'I'll be a queen all right,' she said to King Alfonso XIII of Spain. 'And I'll be it splendidly. For that's the way I believe queens ought to be.' She was as good as her word. Like all actresses, she knew the importance of the right setting, and she presented herself to visitors, in sumptuous rooms that were vaguely Byzantine, with vaulted ceilings glimmering with gold leaf and hung with golden lamps on heavy chains. Great bronze vases filled with white lilies stood on mosaic floors, and divans piled with tiger skins and vermilion cushions lined walls crowded with painted panels and jewelled icons. Her vivacity was extraordinary, her charm overwhelming, and her beauty

(Top) *Marie always enjoyed dressing herself and her children in Romanian national costume. Here she is seen with Prince Carol, Princess Marie and Prince Nicolas.*

(Bottom) *During Queen Marie's tour of the United States in 1926, she was adopted into the Sioux nation by Chief Red Tomahawk, who presented her with the war headdress as a tribute to her courage.*

magnetic. But she was more than just a fascinating cipher: she took her royal duties seriously, and served her country conscientiously and well. And she established an international reputation as a writer of quality. Her massive three-volume autobiography is perhaps the best ever published by a royal writer, and her novels and children's books, though rather too exotic for present-day tastes, display wit, imagination and a remarkable, if overblown, use of language. In the 1920s, Marie also began to write popular journalism, and articles with titles like *My Experiences with Men*, *Making Marriage Durable* and *How It Feels to be a Queen* were syndicated in newspapers all over the world. In 1926 she made a two month tour of the United States, where she was preceded by extravagant publicity and rapturously received by fascinated crowds wherever she went.

Queen Marie's later years were dogged by increasing unhappiness. Her son, Carol, proved to be feckless and irresponsible, and his unfortunate marriage to a Romanian commoner, Zizi Lambrino, and his public liaison with Elena Lupescu scandalised Europe and appalled his mother. Carol's second marriage, to Princess Helen of Greece, was dynastically respectable and produced an heir to the throne, but it was unhappy and ended in divorce. Marie's two elder daughters made glittering but miserable marriages – Elisabeth became Queen of Greece and Marie became Queen of Yugoslavia – and her younger son, Nicolas, married a divorced commoner described by Queen Marie as 'a hardhearted, painted little hussy.' Her youngest daughter, Ileana, married an Austrian archduke, but they were divorced, and she became a Russian Orthodox nun in Pennsylvania, where she lived until her death in 1991. A third son, Mircea, died in 1916 of typhoid, aged three.

The worst was to come when King Ferdinand died in 1927 and Carol became King. It was then that Carol took his revenge on his mother by humiliating her as much as possible. She was kept away from court, consulted on nothing, and allowed no contact with her grandson, the future King Michael. Carol even denied her money, so that she had to live almost entirely on the royalties from her books. But she remained elegant and beautiful into her sixties when a mysterious illness claimed her and she died in 1938. It was just as well that she did not live to see the disintegration of so much that she had loved as the Romanian monarchy was swept away in the political turbulence that followed the Second World War.

Marie in her Byzantine boudoir, with Prince Nicolas (top) *and as Queen Mother of Romania* (centre and below), *still glamorous in her sixties.*

Victoria Melita,
Grand Duchess Kirill of Russia
1876–1936

Princess Victoria Melita was born a year after her sister, Marie, but she was always assumed to be the older of the two. Tall and statuesque, with striking blue eyes and an imperious manner, Victoria Melita lacked the more conventional prettiness of Marie and their younger sisters, but she possessed a regal dignity that, in the words of one observer, 'made her outshine every other woman in the room; strangers immediately asked who she was.'

For all her faults, the Duchess of Edinburgh was a fond and attentive parent, and Victoria Melita – known as Ducky in the family – enjoyed a happy childhood in Kent and Malta, where her father was Commander of Her Majesty's Mediterranean Fleet. She and Marie were devoted to each other and shared an enthusiasm for painting and for riding. They particularly loved Malta where they rode Barbary Arabs to their hearts' content and relished the exotic landscape and flora of the island. But even in these tranquil surroundings, Ducky was to display the temperament that was to figure so largely in her later life: the jealousy, melancholy and inability to tolerate weakness in others or forgive injustice.

The family's move to Coburg in 1889 did not disrupt the close relationship of Ducky and Marie or their delight in horses and painting. Marriage did. When Marie was married in that year to Crown Prince Ferdinand of Romania, Ducky was left in Coburg, resentful, jealous and lonely. And so, when her father and Queen Victoria proposed that she should marry her first cousin, Ernst Ludwig of Hesse, she raised no objections. Even though the match seemed ideal, neither the bride nor the groom were much in favour of it. Ducky and Ernie were the best of friends and shared the same interests, but he was not attracted to women and, by this time, Ducky was already in love with another cousin.

The Grand Duke Kirill Vladimirovitch of Russia was the second son of the Grand Duke Vladimir, Ducky's uncle. Tall, handsome and

Princess Victoria Melita lacked the conventional prettiness of her sister but, even as a child, she possessed a regal dignity.

aristocratic, Kirill was far better suited to Ducky than the mercurial and sensitive Ernie, but not everyone shared Ducky's admiration for him. Her sister, Marie, thought him cold and selfish, with a disdainful manner that was often intimidating. A marriage between Ducky and Kirill was out of the question because the Russian Orthodox church did not allow such unions between first cousins, but this restriction did not apply to the Protestant faith, and Ducky and Ernie were obediently if unwillingly married in Darmstadt in 1894.

Despite the birth of their daughter, Elisabeth, in 1895, and the liveliness of their social life, the marriage of Ducky and Ernie was a failure. And Ducky failed, too, in her rôle as Grand Duchess of Hesse. She refused to conform to the standards of conduct expected of her and neglected her official duties, often disappearing for hours on end on her favourite black stallion.

In 1901, the death of Queen Victoria allowed Ducky and Ernie to end their marriage at last, and in December of that year they were divorced. Four years later Ducky and Kirill were secretly married in her mother's private chapel at Coburg. Ducky's second marriage precipitated a scandal that eclipsed the sensation of her divorce. Ducky's royal relations were appalled by her action, none more so than the Empress Alexandra, Ernie's sister. Eight years earlier, Ducky's marriage to Ernie had encouraged Alix to marry Nicholas and leave home; now she was expected to receive Ducky at her court. Alix was deeply religious and it seemed to her intolerable that she should be required to receive the divorced wife of her own brother. She insisted that the Tsar disown and banish Kirill and Ducky. Tsar Nicholas was reluctant to take this course – Kirill was, after all, his cousin, and Nicholas himself had been a regular guest at those boisterous weekend parties in Darmstadt – but he nonetheless stripped Kirill of his rank, decorations and privileges, and gave him forty-eight hours to leave Russia. The rest of the Imperial family were horrified, especially Kirill's parents. The Grand Duke Vladimir flung his own decorations in the Tsar's face, and the Imperial Palace echoed with noisy scenes between the Empress and Kirill's mother. Ducky and Kirill, meanwhile, retreated into exile, where they were supported financially by her mother and his parents, and divided their time between homes in Paris, Nice and Munich. It was not until the death of Grand Duke Vladimir, in 1909, that Kirill was reinstated and allowed to return to Russia.

Victoria Melita and Prince Ernst Ludwig of Hesse at the time of their engagement (above)*, and on their wedding day in 1894* (below).

It was then that Ducky at last came into her own. The magnificence of the Imperial Court was the setting she needed, and she relished the

Victoria Melita and her daughter,
Princess Elisabeth, taken in 1898.
Elisabeth died in 1903, aged eight.

spectacular social life of St Petersburg and the elaborate ceremonial and splendid pageantry of the court. Alix watched resentfully as Ducky became the leader of St Petersburg society, the glittering instigator of elaborate parties and magnificent balls. She gave splendid picnics in the countryside, with liveried servants to serve exotic food and orchestras to entertain the guests. She hired a skating rink and held a

Victoria Melita seen shortly before the
First World War, with her daughters,
Princess Kira (left) *and Princess Maria.*

ball on roller skates. Society revolved around her as the last years of Tsarist Russia drew to a close.

Despite their delight in the more frivolous world of the court, Ducky and Kirill were well aware of the growing unrest in the country. With other members of the Imperial family they pleaded with the Tsar for the removal of Rasputin. But he and Alix ignored them and, at last, the glittering court and the society that fluttered round it crumbled and collapsed in 1917.

Ducky and Kirill fared better than most under Kerensky's provisional government, and because of their initial opposition to the Tsar they were spared death. But they were imprisoned in their palace and deprived of their wealth. In Romania, Queen Marie could only watch helplessly as her beloved sister's world collapsed.

It soon became clear that Ducky and Kirill could no longer expect to avoid the fate of the rest of their family, and they left St Petersburg for Finland with their two daughters, Maria and Kira. A romantic legend has grown up around their escape. It has been said that Kirill carried the pregnant Ducky across the ice of the frozen Gulf of Finland to safety, and that they starved there for two years in a small wooden house, chopping up the doors and window frames for firewood. The truth is far less dramatic. The family left St Petersburg by train, with several servants and with the permission of the authorities, and spent their time in Finland living on the estate of old family friends. It was there that their only son, Vladimir, was born.

From Finland Ducky and Kirill moved to St Briac in Brittany, where he proclaimed himself 'Guardian of the Throne', rightful heir to the crown of the Romanovs. This caused great dissension among the ranks of Russian emigrés, who claimed that Kirill was not eligible for the throne because he had married a divorced woman without permission, and that she had only converted to the Russian Orthodox faith some time after their marriage. Besides, there were other surviving Grand Dukes who were just as eligible as he was. Kirill persisted in his claim, however, and he occupied his exile by issuing Imperial directives and decrees. Kirill's son, the Grand Duke Vladimir, succeeded his father as Head of the Imperial House of Russia in 1938.

In the 1930s, Ducky lent her support to the Nazi movement, in the belief that it offered the best hope of a Romanov restoration. It has also been claimed that she donated large sums of money to Nazi funds and gave some of her jewels to Hitler. And it was at this time, also, that she discovered that Kirill had been unfaithful to her for years. Those few brilliant, happy years in Russia had, after all, been a mockery. In 1936 Ducky died at her daughter's house in Bavaria. Her sister Marie was there to lay white lilacs on Ducky's body. 'She was the proudest, strongest, most upright, most capable, most law-abiding but also the most unforgiving of us all,' Marie wrote afterwards. 'It was this inability to forgive which finally broke her. She had no understanding for weakness, could not accept compromise of any kind. Her ideals were absolute, not to be discussed. There was something of Lucifer's pride about her – magnificent but dangerous.'

Victoria Melita's second husband, Grand Duke Kirill of Russia (top) *and* (below) *the exiled Victoria Melita, taken shortly before her death in 1936.*

Princess Alexandra's mother considered her 'the most uninteresting specimen' among her daughters. She is seen (above) with Prince Ernst of Hohenlohe-Langenburg at the time of their wedding in 1896.

Alexandra, Princess of Hohenlohe-Langenburg
1878–1942

Of the four Edinburgh princesses, it was Alexandra who was the least prepossessing, and even her mother thought her 'the most uninteresting specimen' of her daughters. Sandra, as she was known, was well aware of her lack of distinction, and although she was lucky enough to lead a more harmonious and contented life than her sisters, she nonetheless resented their more brilliant positions and was often jealous, bad-tempered and ill as a result.

In 1896, Sandra married Prince Ernst of Hohenlohe-Langenburg, a grandson of Queen Victoria's half-sister. The wedding took place against the wishes of Sandra's father and her sister, Marie, who considered the match to be less than distinguished. Compared with those of her sisters, Sandra's husband was, indeed, less important in terms of position and royal rank, but her home in the picturesque Schloss Langenburg, perched on a green mountain ridge near Hesse, became a haven of peace for her Romanian nephews and nieces, who were glad to escape there occasionally from the more turbulent court in Bucharest. On the death of Sandra's father in 1900, Ernst became Regent of the duchy of Saxe-Coburg and Gotha during the minority of the new Duke, Prince Charles Edward, Duke of Albany, who was then sixteen.

Sandra and Ernst had five children. The eldest, Gottfried, married Princess Margarita of Greece, the eldest sister of Prince Philip, Duke of Edinburgh. Their second daughter, Marie Melita, married Prince Friedrich of Schleswig-Holstein-Sonderburg-Glucksburg, but their two younger daughters, Alexandra and Irma, never married. A second son, Alfred, died two days after his birth in 1911.

Sandra was an early supporter of the ideals of Adolf Hitler but she died in 1942, without seeing the final destruction of Nazi Germany.

Beatrice, Infanta of Spain 1884–1966

The youngest of the Duke of Edinburgh's daughters was born in 1884, six years after her sister, Alexandra. Because she was so much younger than the others, Princess Beatrice was always known as Baby Bee, a nickname which remained with her all her life.

Baby Bee grew to be a striking young woman, and when the unmarried King Alfonso XIII of Spain visited England in 1905, she was considered as a possible bride for him. But in the end, it was the cool blonde beauty of Ena of Battenberg that the King preferred, and they were married the following year. Baby Bee was never to forgive her cousin for being the King's choice.

Baby Bee's own Spanish marriage to the charming Infante Alfonso, a first cousin of the King, met with strong disapproval in her adopted country. This objection was primarily religious, for Baby Bee was not a Roman Catholic at the time of her wedding. Alfonso was deprived of his royal privileges and banished from Spain. Baby Bee and Alfonso spent the years of their exile in Switzerland, until his privileges were restored by royal decree in 1912 and they were able to return to Spain.

Baby Bee quickly became the supposed confidante of her cousin, Queen Ena. At the same time she caught the notoriously roving eye of the King and, although he and Baby Bee were never lovers, as was commonly supposed, she did flirt outrageously with him whenever Ena was looking. She also introduced him to a succession of attractive mistresses. The King's promiscuity, and Baby Bee's encouragement of it, soon began to cause concern in the royal family, and at last the Dowager Queen Maria Cristina was forced to ask her to leave the country. She refused, and then the King himself ordered her to go.

Baby Bee and Alfonso, together with their sons, Alvaro, Alonso and Ataulfo, moved to England where they took up residence in Esher. The Infante Alfonso worked for a time with the Ford Motor Company, and the young princes went to school at Winchester College. In later years, Baby Bee and her family were able to return to Spain, where she died in 1966.

Princess Beatrice as a child (above) *and with her own children, Prince Alvaro, Prince Ataulfo (as a baby) and Prince Alonso* (below).

The Children of Helena and Christian

Christian Victor
Prince of Schleswig-Holstein
1867–1900

Albert
Duke of Schleswig-Holstein
1869–1931

Helena Victoria
Princess of Schleswig-Holstein
1870–1948

Marie Louise
Princess of Schleswig-Holstein
1872–1956

Harold
Prince of Schleswig-Holstein
1876

Helena
& Christian of
Schleswig-Holstein

Princess Helena – always known as Lenchen – was born in 1846. Unlike her more mercurial elder sisters, she was a plain and placid child with no aptitude for study and little interest in conventional feminine accomplishments. She enjoyed outdoor pursuits and working with machines, but her abiding passion was riding, and she had an instinctive ability to manage and control horses. Prince Albert encouraged her mechanical skills, and insisted that she groom and muck out her horses herself.

After Prince Albert's death, Lenchen's even temper and unemotional character were a constant support to Queen Victoria, who expected this awkward daughter to remain at home to be a comfort to her in her widowhood. Prince Albert, though, had hoped that Lenchen would marry, and the Queen reluctantly agreed to abide by his wishes and find her a suitable husband who would be content to live in England.

The successful candidate was Prince Christian of Schleswig-Holstein-Sonderburg-Augustenburg, a poor, disinherited younger son with no prospects in Germany and every interest in marrying a daughter of Queen Victoria. He was balding, unprepossessing, and fifteen years older than Lenchen, but their marriage was long and happy. Lenchen and Christian were well suited, and he was quite content to spend his days performing mundane tasks and reading aloud to Queen Victoria. In 1891, he was accidentally shot in the eye by his brother-in-law, the Duke of Connaught. The eye had to be removed, and it is said that Prince Christian would then take his pick from a selection of glass eyes, including one that was bloodshot.

Despite the fact that she had a family and commitments of her own, Lenchen was expected to assist and accompany the Queen whenever she was required to do so. As well as these duties, she took an active interest in nursing organisations and shared with her sisters a deep love of music. Lenchen and Christian celebrated their Golden Wedding in 1916, a year before his death. Lenchen lived on until 1923.

The four children of Princess Helena and Prince Christian. (Above) *Princess Helena Victoria (behind)* with Prince Christian Victor, Princess Marie Louise and Prince Albert. (Right) *Prince Christian Victor (left)* with Prince Albert.

Prince Christian Victor of Schleswig-Holstein
1867–1900

Princess Helena's first child was born at Windsor Castle in 1867, a year after her marriage. Prince Christian Victor was by all accounts a pleasant and charming young man, devoted to his family and his dogs and admired by all who knew him. He made a successful career in the Army, becoming a Captain in the 60th King's Royal Rifles. He served under Kitchener in the Sudan and with his uncle, Prince Henry of Battenberg, in the Ashanti Expedition of 1895, before setting off to South Africa to serve with the British Army in the Boer War. Three weeks before he was due to return home, the prince contracted enteric fever, and he died in Pretoria in 1900.

The news of Prince Christian Victor's death came as an enormous shock to his family, particularly to his mother, who idolised him, and to his adoring sister, Princess Helena Victoria. But onlookers were taken aback by the intensity of the grief of Queen Victoria. Prince Christian Victor was the third of her adult grandsons to die – his cousins Albert Victor of Wales and Alfred of Edinburgh had predeceased him – but the Queen had been particularly close to this likeable and devoted prince, and she had still not recovered from the shock of the death of her own son, the Duke of Edinburgh, just over two months before. The Queen did not long outlive Prince Christian Victor, for she died some two months later, on 22 January, 1901.

Prince Christian Victor, taken shortly before his death during the Boer War in 1900.

Albert, Duke of Schleswig-Holstein
1869–1931

Prince Albert, aged twenty, at the time he became heir to the Dukedom of Schleswig-Holstein-Sonderburg-Augustenburg.

Like his cousins, Alfred of Edinburgh and Charles Edward of Albany, Prince Albert of Schleswig-Holstein went to live in Germany when it was agreed that he would inherit the Dukedom of Schleswig-Holstein-Sonderburg-Augustenburg on the death of his childless cousin, Duke Ernst Gunther. He served in the Prussian Army but, by all accounts, he was a reluctant soldier. In 1889, Queen Victoria told her daughter, Vicky, that Albert 'hates the sight of a soldier and can't bear being on horseback and is to go into a cavalry regiment.'

Albert never married, but he was the father of Princess Helena's only grandchild, Valerie Marie, who was born in Hungary in 1900. It is unlikely that Princess Helena ever knew of the existence of her granddaughter, and Albert never revealed the identity of the child's mother. Valerie Marie was brought up by a Jewish family and she knew little of her true parentage until she received a letter from Albert shortly before his death in 1931. She then changed her name to zu Schleswig-Holstein. This change was necessary on her second marriage in 1939 to Duke Engelbert-Charles of Arenberg. Nazi law prohibited mixed marriages, and it was essential for Valerie Marie to prove that she was not Jewish like her foster-parents. Her aunts, Princesses Helena Victoria and Marie Louise, signed a letter acknowledging their niece and testifying that she was Aryan.

When the First World War was declared, Albert felt obliged to place his services at the disposal of the German Emperor, on condition that he should not be sent to serve on the Western Front. All the same, like his cousins, he was distressed to find himself on the opposing side to so many members of his family.

Albert succeeded to the Dukedom of Schleswig-Holstein on the death, in 1921, of Duke Ernst Gunther, and he himself died in Berlin ten years later. The Augustenburg line of the Ducal House then became extinct.

Princess Helena Victoria
1870–1948

The full name of Princess Helena's third child and elder daughter was Victoria Louise Sophia Augusta Amelia Helena, but she was always known as Princess Helena Victoria. Her family nickname was Thora, which derived from her sister's inability to pronounce 'Victoria' when she was a child, and she was known behind her back as 'The Snipe', because of her long nose and doleful expression.

Although they were very different in temperament and character, Princess Thora and her younger sister, Marie Louise, were devoted to each other and, apart from the ten years of Marie Louise's unhappy marriage, they were inseparable companions from early childhood until Thora's death in 1948. Their early life was spent at the family homes – Cumberland Lodge in Windsor Great Park and Buckingham Palace – under the care of German and French governesses, and they spent each summer at Darmstadt with their Hessian cousins. It appears that Thora's tendency to bossiness could be annoying at times, for Queen Victoria once advised another granddaughter, Victoria of Hesse, to 'sit upon' Thora a little and not to 'let her be forward and try to dictate'.

Thora grew into a sensible, level-headed and intelligent young woman, but she was not pretty, and eligible royal suitors failed to present themselves, despite the valiant efforts of her mother to arrange a suitable marriage. Princess Helena had hoped that Prince Albert Victor of Wales would marry one of her daughters, and she was extremely offended when both Thora and Marie Louise were passed over in favour of Princess May of Teck. There was a great deal of ill-feeling in the royal family for a time as a result, but this disappointment did not prevent Princess Helena from deciding that Albert Victor's brother, George, would be a suitable alternative. 'So the Christians have been following you about with their lovely Snipe,' the Princess of Wales wrote wickedly to her son. 'Well, it will be a pleasure to welcome that beauty as your bride. When may we expect the

Princess Helena Victoria at the age of three, pictured with her mother, Princess Helena, in 1873.

news?' But George was not interested in Thora either. Princess Helena and Queen Victoria then looked further afield for a possible husband, assisted as always by Vicky, who was better placed than they to advise on the particular merits of German princelings. For a time it seemed as though the Prince of Hohenlohe-Bartenstein might be suitable, but there was a difference of religion, and Thora, practical as ever, wanted this difficulty to be sorted out well in advance in order to avoid any future disappointment should she take a definite liking to the prince. But nothing came of this match, either. Thora never married, much to her own disappointment and that of her friends, who felt that she would have made an ideal royal consort. One of Queen Victoria's ladies-in-waiting remarked that 'it would have been a godsend to Russia if the Tsar had married her instead of the angelic but somewhat cow-like princess whom he adores.'

Helena Victoria was known behind her back as 'The Snipe', because of her long nose and doleful expression.

Thora now resigned herself to a life of charitable works, acting as bridesmaid at the weddings of her cousins, and being an unpaid companion to her mother and, from time to time, Queen Victoria. It was on one of these occasions that her choice of dress breached the Queen's limits of decorum. One evening, as the royal party were about to enter the dining room, Queen Victoria gestured towards Thora's décolletage and remarked, 'A little rose in front, dear child, because of the footmen.'

Both Thora and Marie Louise inherited from their mother a deep love and appreciation of music, and their later home together, Schomberg House in Pall Mall, became a renowned centre for private concerts and musical evenings. The princess also enjoyed golf, riding and hunting. Her greatest charitable interests were the Y.M.C.A., the Docklands Settlement, and the Women's Auxiliary Force, which she formed during the First World War. She spent much of the war years visiting hospitals in France, and arranging musical entertainment for the troops on the Western Front.

When George V abolished all the royal family's German titles in 1917, Thora and Marie Louise lost the designation Schleswig-Holstein but retained the title Princess. In this they were more fortunate than their Teck and Battenberg cousins, who lost all their royal attributes. Thora last appeared in public at the wedding of the present Queen in 1947, when she could be seen sitting in a wheelchair, prodding Prince Richard of Gloucester with her stick. She died three months later.

Princess Marie Louise

1872–1956

Princess Marie Louise was born at Cumberland Lodge in 1872 and, like her sister before her, she was given an impressive array of names. Queen Victoria, as always, had her own ideas on this subject and told Princess Helena that the child should be called Georgina. As the infant princess already had seven names, her parents politely refused, and their daughter was known as Marie Louise, in honour of the Emperor Napoleon's second wife, whom Prince Christian had once escorted into dinner at the age of eleven and adored ever afterwards. Her nickname in the family was Louie.

Louie was livelier and more vivacious than her sister but, like Thora, she was not conventionally pretty. As a baby, the princess had been thought 'excessively plain' by Queen Victoria, and her opinion had not changed a year later when she sent a telegram to Louie's absent parents which read: 'Children very well but poor little Louise very ugly.' The princess, too, became well-known for her forthright opinions. Once, when her parents' friend, the Swedish singer Jenny Lind, had given a special performance for her and her brothers and sister in their nursery, Louie went up to her and asked, 'Must you always make such a noise when you sing?'

In 1890, Louie and her family went to Berlin for the wedding of her cousin, Princess Viktoria of Prussia, and it was there that she met Prince Aribert of Anhalt, the fourth son of the reigning Duke of a minor German principality. Louie fell in love with him and they became engaged, with the direct encouragement of her cousin, Wilhelm II. Louie was certainly a splendid catch for such an unimportant prince, and the Anhalt family were delighted at this alliance with the family of Queen Victoria. Louie, for her part, was greatly attracted to the dashing young prince who, according to another observer, was 'extremely good looking even for a Prince, tall and slim with a sufficiency of chin'.

Louie and Aribert were married in St George's Chapel, Windsor, in

Princess Marie Louise in 1893, two years after her marriage to Prince Aribert of Anhalt.

Princess Marie Louise. As a child she had been considered to be 'very ugly' by her grandmother, Queen Victoria.

July 1891 and left shortly afterwards for their new home in Berlin. The next nine years were to be increasingly unhappy for Louie, as it became apparent early on that the marriage had been a mistake. Although she may have been devoted to Aribert, he had no feelings at all towards her. She soon realised that there was no companionship between them and that her presence annoyed him. 'We occasionally met at meals and when we had guests,' she wrote later, 'otherwise days might pass without our ever seeing each other.'

In 1900, Louie left Germany for a private visit to the United States and Canada, and it was while she was in Ottawa that she received a summons from Queen Victoria to return immediately to England. When she arrived, she learned that Aribert had asked his father to exercise his right as a sovereign prince and declare the marriage null and void. Louie was never to understand why this was done, and she would never acknowledge that her marriage had, indeed, ended. To her, the vows she had made at her wedding were indissoluble. The Anhalt family presented various unconvincing reasons for ending the marriage, including Louie's childlessness and her fondness for England, but the real cause was scrupulously concealed: Prince Aribert had been discovered in a compromising situation with another man. Both families wished to avoid scandal at all costs, and so it had been decided that the news should be given out that the marriage had been ended by mutual agreement. The true circumstances were never revealed but rumours abounded. It was said, for instance, that Aribert had squandered all Louie's money and seized her jewellery.

Louie settled down with her sister Thora and tried to put the years of her marriage behind her. She devoted the rest of her life to convivial friendships and to charitable causes, which ranged from hospitals, girls' clubs and the Church Army to 'Pearly Kings' and the British Empire Shakespeare Society. She became proficient at enamelling in precious metals, collected Napoleonic relics, and spent a great deal of time travelling in Africa, the West Indies and the Far East.

In 1956, when she was eighty-four years old, Louie published a volume of autobiography, *My Memories of Six Reigns*, which was an immediate best-seller. She died a few weeks later at her home in Mayfair.

Princess Marie Louise with Prince Aribert at the time of their wedding in 1891. He was considered to be 'extremely good looking, even for a prince', but the marriage was not a success.

Prince Harold of Schleswig-Holstein
1876

A third son, Frederick Christian Augustus Edward Harold, was born to Princess Helena on 12 May, 1876, at Cumberland Lodge. The infant prince, who was known as Prince Harold, lived for only eight days.

The Children of Arthur and Luise Margarete

Margaret
Crown Princess of Sweden
1882–1920

Arthur
Prince of Connaught
1883–1938

Patricia
Lady Patricia Ramsay
1886–1974

Arthur & Luise Margarete of Prussia

Prince Arthur, the third son of Queen Victoria, was born on the eighty-first birthday of his godfather, the Duke of Wellington, after whom he was named. The Queen was later to write that Arthur had never given her a day's trouble, and he soon became her favourite son.

From an early age, Arthur displayed a deep interest in military matters, and he became an expert in British and Prussian army regiments and the careers of Napoleon and Wellington. It was only to be expected that he would enter the Army as soon as he was old enough and, after two years at the Royal Military Academy at Woolwich, he was commissioned into the Royal Engineers and later transferred to the Rifle Brigade. During a long and successful military career, he served in Canada, Egypt and India, where he became fluent in Hindustani. He became a General in 1893, and was promoted to the rank of Field Marshal nine years later. He was created Duke of Connaught in 1874.

In 1879, Prince Arthur married Princess Luise Margarete of Prussia, with whom he had fallen in love seven years earlier, when she was twelve. Queen Victoria did not at first approve of the match, mainly because she did not see why Arthur should marry at all or, if he did, why he had to choose the plain daughter of a tyrannical prince whose violent treatment of his wife and family was a scandal in royal circles. After the marriage, though, the Queen revised her opinion and formed a close relationship with Luise. Arthur proved to be a loving and considerate husband and father, and his life was untouched by scandal. He enjoyed a close but discreet friendship with Leonie Lady Leslie, the sister of Lady Randolph Churchill, who was also a close friend of his wife.

Luise died in 1917, and Arthur never fully recovered from the shock. In 1926, he became a godfather of the present Queen and two years later he retired from public life. Prince Arthur died in 1942, at the age of ninety-one, the last surviving son of Queen Victoria.

A family group (above) *at the christening of Princess Margaret's first child. Seated,* (left to right) *are the Duke of Connaught, Princess Margaret with her baby son, and her mother, the Duchess of Connaught. Standing,* (left to right) *are Princess Patricia, Prince Arthur and Prince Gustaf Adolf. Princess Margaret's second son, Sigvord, was born in 1907, and is seen* (top right) *with his mother and elder brother, Gustaf Adolf. The two princes were joined in 1910 by a sister, Ingrid, pictured* (right) *with her brothers. In 1935, Princess Ingrid married Crown Prince Frederick of Denmark, and became Queen in 1947.*

Margaret, Crown Princess of Sweden
1882–1920

The Connaughts were a devoted and popular family, and Margaret – or Daisy, as she was known – was particularly liked by everyone. Queen Victoria was known for her dislike of babies but even she was charmed by the infant Daisy, and as an adult, Daisy retained her charm and popularity.

It is hardly surprising, then, that this attractive and appealing princess should excite the admiration of foreign princes in search of a suitable bride. Among them was Prince Gustaf Adolf, the eldest son of the Crown Prince of Sweden. They became engaged in Cairo, where the Duke of Connaught was serving at the time, and were married in St George's Chapel, Windsor, in June 1905.

Gustaf Adolf was a pleasing and popular prince who, according to the Princess of Pless, was 'one of the nicest royalties in Europe.' He was also modest and well-mannered, and his progressive political ideas endeared him to his people when he became king. He and Daisy were a devoted and popular couple.

Daisy's arrival in Sweden was not universally popular at first. Although the Swedish dynasty was French in origin it had become thoroughly German in character by the time of Daisy's arrival. But Daisy's charm soon earned her the love and respect of the royal family and the Swedish people, and any resentment was quickly forgotten.

When the First World War broke out, the pro-German sentiments of the royal family made Daisy's life difficult at times but, even so, she was able to set up an organisation to locate and identify British wounded and prisoners-of-war in Germany and pass messages and assistance to them.

In 1920, Daisy died suddenly of peritonitis while she was expecting her sixth child. The country was shocked by the unexpected early death of the popular Crown Princess, and she was deeply mourned. Three years later, Crown Prince Gustaf Adolf married Lady Louise Mountbatten.

Princess Margaret shortly before her sudden death in 1920. Three years later, Crown Prince Gustaf Adolf was married again to Lady Louise Mountbatten, daughter of Victoria, Marchioness of Milford Haven.

Prince Arthur of Connaught

1883–1938

Prince Arthur (above) followed his father's example and made the army his career. The prince is seen (below) with his sister, Princess Patricia, his mother and the Duke of Connaught.

It was perhaps only to be expected that the Duke of Connaught's only son would follow his father's example and make the army his career. In 1899, however, the death of Prince Arthur's cousin, Prince Alfred of Saxe-Coburg and Gotha, threatened to change the predictable course of his life.

Prince Alfred's early death left the Duke of Saxe-Coburg without an heir. The succession now passed to the Duke's younger brother, the Duke of Connaught, and his son, Prince Arthur. The Duke of Connaught declined the position for himself because of his army career, but both he and the Duke of Saxe-Coburg were anxious for Prince Arthur to inherit. Arthur, then a fifteen-year-old Eton schoolboy, did not take kindly to the idea. It is said that he then sought out his fellow Etonian, Prince Charles Edward, Duke of Albany, the only son of the Duke of Connaught's younger brother, Leopold. Prince Charles Edward was next in line to the succession of Saxe-Coburg, and the story goes that Arthur threatened to thrash his cousin unless he agreed to become the heir to the Duchy. Whether this story is true or not, it was indeed finally agreed that Charles Edward would inherit the dukedom, and he went to live in Germany with his mother and sister.

Prince Arthur continued his education at Eton and went from there to the Royal Military College at Sandhurst. In 1901 he joined the 7th Hussars and served in South Africa and later fought in the First World War, when he was twice mentioned in despatches. He also undertook various ceremonial missions abroad on behalf of the King. The Prince was appointed Personal A.D.C. to every British sovereign from Edward VII to George VI, and from 1920 to 1924 he served as Governor-General of South Africa.

In 1913, Arthur married Princess Alexandra, Duchess of Fife, the elder daughter of his first cousin, Princess Louise. Princess Alexandra devoted most of her life to nursing and served in London hospitals during both world wars. She later became the formidable matron of her

Prince Arthur as a small boy (right) *with his cousins Alice and Charles Edward of Albany* (in pram) *and his sister Margaret. (Below)* Prince Arthur's wife, Princess Alexandra, Duchess of Fife, with their son, Prince Alistair, who succeeded his grandfather as Duke of Connaught.

own nursing home, which she ran for ten years until rheumatoid arthritis forced her to retire. Arthur and Alexandra had one son, Prince Alastair, who was born in 1914.

Prince Arthur was pleasant, undemanding and courteous, and he was once described by Princess Daisy of Pless as 'such a nice intelligent boy overflowing with sensible conversation.' There were some, though, whose opinion of the Prince was less enthusiastic. Lord Esher once described him as being a 'very amiable but silly goose' and told his son after a visit to Balmoral that Arthur was 'very chancy in his kilt – sits in odd positions – and shows everything he has to show, which is not much.'

In 1938, Prince Arthur died of cancer, four years before his father. Arthur's son, Alastair, became the second Duke of Connaught on his grandfather's death in 1942. Alastair had lost the title of Prince in 1917, when he was three. In that year, George V had limited the use of royal styles and titles, and so Alastair was created Earl of Macduff instead. He grew to be a pleasant but completely irresponsible young man, and he died suddenly of hypothermia in 1943 while staying with his father's cousin, Princess Alice, Countess of Athlone, in Ottawa. Alastair was unmarried and the Dukedom of Connaught became extinct on his death.

Lady Patricia Ramsay

1886–1974

The popular Princess Patricia (above) was known affectionately as Princess Pat. She is seen (below) with her infant son, Alexander.

Queen Victoria's twentieth granddaughter was born on St Patrick's Day, 1886, and although her first name was Victoria she was always called Patricia in honour of the day of her birth. To the country at large, though, this popular princess was always known affectionately as Princess Pat, and to her family she was simply Patsy.

Patricia grew to be tall and beautiful, and she developed a remarkable talent for painting in oils, water colour and gouache. Her early subjects were flowers and marine life, but she later turned to more abstract themes. Although she completed over six hundred paintings, she exhibited her work very rarely and refused to allow it to be hung at the Royal Academy.

Like her sister, Daisy, Princess Patricia was seen as an ideal candidate for a spectacular foreign marriage. In 1903, the Grand Duke Vladimir of Russia visited England to press the suit of his son, Grand Duke Kirill, who, it was said, had fallen violently in love with Patricia. This may have been wishful thinking on Vladimir's part, for Kirill by this time was already in love with Patricia's unsuitable cousin, Victoria Melita. Two years later, the nineteen-year-old King Alfonso of Spain came to England on a state visit, and it was generally agreed that the primary purpose of Alfonso's visit was to propose to her. It soon became apparent, though, that Patricia was not in the least interested in the King, whose usually irresistible charm made no impact on her whatsoever. But Alfonso was not discouraged for long; he turned his attention instead to Patricia's more amenable cousins and fell in love with 'the fair one', Princess Ena of Battenberg.

In 1911, Patricia accompanied her parents to Canada when the Duke of Connaught was appointed Governor-General. She soon became as popular there as she was in England, and in 1914 she became Colonel-in-Chief of Princess Patricia's Canadian Light Infantry. She personally embroidered the colour that the regiment carried into battle, and she remained their Colonel-in-Chief until her death.

It was in Canada that Princess Patricia fell in love with the Hon. Alexander Ramsay, a young naval officer who was an aide-de-camp to her father. Although Alexander was the third son of the Earl of Dalhousie, a marriage between him and Patricia could not be considered, for no princess of the Blood Royal had ever married a commoner without a hereditary peerage. It has been said that Patricia's mother was sympathetic to their romance and that it was her father who strenuously opposed it. Other sources have claimed that it was the Duchess who was antagonistic. In any event, it was only after her mother's death, and the accession of King George V, that Patricia at last obtained permission for her marriage to take place.

Princess Patricia's wedding, in February 1919, was an occasion of great national celebration. Not only was Princess Pat marrying a commoner but, for the first time since 1296, a royal wedding was held in Westminster Abbey. Two days before her marriage, Princess Patricia relinquished by Royal Warrant all her royal titles and privileges. From then on she was to be known simply as Lady Patricia Ramsay.

Although she remained an active member of the royal family and appeared at state and family celebrations, Patricia led a quiet life out of the public eye. In 1919, her only child, Alexander, was born. Patricia's husband was knighted in 1937 and retired with the rank of Admiral in 1942. In that same year he and Patricia went to live near Windlesham in Surrey. It was there that Alexander died in 1972. By the time that Patricia died, two years later, the popular Princess Pat of sixty years before had become virtually unknown to the people of Britain.

Princess Patricia, now Lady Patricia Ramsay, returning from Westminster Abbey after her wedding in 1919 (left). *Her marriage was the first royal wedding to take place in the Abbey since 1296. She is seen* (below) *with her father, the Duke of Connaught, her husband, the Hon. Alexander Ramsay, and their son Alexander.*

The Children of Leopold and Helene

Alice
Countess of Athlone
1883–1981

Charles Edward
Duke of Saxe-Coburg and Gotha
1884–1954

Leopold
& Helene of
Waldeck-Pyrmont

Queen Victoria's fourth son, born in 1853, was the first of her descendants to suffer from haemophilia, the malady which was to scar the lives of so many of her grandchildren and great-grandchildren. Prince Leopold was three when the disease was diagnosed and this, together with the epilepsy which he developed at an early age, obliged him to lead the life of an invalid.

Although Queen Victoria pampered and cosseted her 'child of anxiety', as she called him, Prince Albert took pains to ensure that his son led as active a life as possible and encouraged, too, Leopold's keen intellect and artistic talents. The Prince was the most gifted of Victoria's sons; he became an expert on early Italian art, a fine pianist, and a skilled linguist. He was also interested in politics and collected geological specimens.

After his father's death, Leopold rebelled against the constraints placed upon him by his mother and led an increasingly independent life. Despite her objections, he went to Oxford University, where he experienced for the first time full physical and intellectual freedom. After leaving university, he set up home on his own, and travelled widely in Europe and Canada, where his sister, Princess Louise, was the wife of the Governor-General. He also led an active social and artistic life in England, becoming President of the Royal Society of Literature. In 1881, he was created Duke of Albany and, in the following year, he married Helene of Waldeck-Pyrmont, an attractive and intelligent princess who was well aware of the implications of Leopold's medical condition. Their first child, Princess Alice, was born ten months later.

In 1884, Leopold travelled as usual to the south of France to escape the rigours of the English winter and died there suddenly after a fall at Cannes. He was thirty years old. Princess Helene, widowed after two years of marriage, devoted the rest of her life to the care and support of her two children. She died in 1922, while visiting her son in Austria.

(Right) *The widowed Duchess of Albany with Princess Alice and Prince Charles Edward in 1889.* (Far right) *Princess Alice and her husband, Prince Alexander of Teck, in 1908.* (Below) *The wedding of Princess Alice and Prince Alexander in 1904. The bridesmaids were* (back row) *Princess Margaret and Princess Patricia of Connaught, and* (front row) *Princess Mary of Wales, daughter of George V; Princess Helen of Waldeck-Pyrmont, the bride's first cousin; and Princess Mary of Teck, the bridegroom's niece.*

Alice, Countess of Athlone
1883–1981

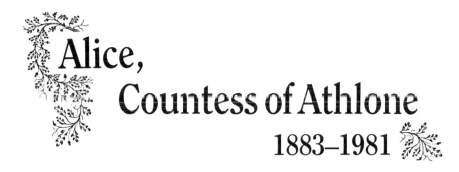

Princess Alice was just thirteen months old when her father died but the lively, artistic spirit of the dead Prince Leopold was to live on in his daughter, who had none of the crippling shyness that afflicted so many of her cousins and who retained her impish zest for life well into old age.

Alice, and her younger brother, Charlie, enjoyed a happy and peaceful childhood at Claremont House, near Esher, which had been given to Prince Leopold by his mother as a wedding present. Although the income of the widowed Duchess of Albany was greatly reduced after Leopold's death, the family circumstances were nonetheless comfortable and privileged. The Duchess of Albany was determined that her children should be brought up with a proper sense of respect for authority, and an understanding of their duties in life as well as their advantages, but her firm tutelage was never severe and allowed plenty of opportunity for fun and relaxation. During their childhood, Alice and her brother saw a great deal of their royal relations, not only in England but in Germany and Holland too. The Albany family paid regular visits to Waldeck, where the Duchess's parents lived, and to The Hague, where her sister, Emma, was Queen of the Netherlands. Queen Victoria took a particularly tender interest in the children of her dead son, and her attitude towards the boisterous Alice was fond and indulgent. She was even known to allow her lively granddaughter to build houses with her despatch boxes as she worked at her desk nearby.

Princess Alice was a boisterous and high-spirited child and she retained her sense of fun throughout her long life.

The Duke and Duchess of Albany had enjoyed the company of many distiguished literary and artistic figures of the day, and this friendship continued after the Duke's death. Among these friends was Lewis Carroll, the author of *Alice's Adventures in Wonderland*, who thought Alice's brother, Charlie, 'a perfect little Prince', but considered his sister to be too high-spirited.

In 1899, when Alice was sixteen, her brother became heir to the

Prince Alexander of Teck (right), *holding his first child, Princess May, with his brother-in-law, the Duke of Saxe-Coburg and Gotha, who is carrying his eldest son, Prince Johann Leopold.*

Duchy of Saxe-Coburg and Gotha. It then became necessary for Charlie to leave Eton and be educated as a German prince, but his mother would not hear of him going to live in Germany alone and so she and Alice accompanied him. The family settled in Potsdam, where Charlie began his military training and Alice attended a finishing school. She and her mother returned to England in 1903, when the Duchess considered that her son could now manage without her.

It was on their return to England that Alice caught the eye of Prince Alexander of Teck, the elder brother of Princess May, who was now Princess of Wales. Alge, as he was known in the family, was a charming and amiable young army officer who had served heroically in India, Matabeleland and South Africa. He was tall and handsome, and had a lively spirit that matched that of Princess Alice. They became engaged at the end of 1903 and were married in St George's Chapel, Windsor, in the following February.

Alge continued with his military service after their marriage, and Princess Alice's first married home was the Royal Pavilion at Aldershot. Later, the King insisted that Alge transfer from the 7th Hussars to the Royal Horse Guards so that he and Alice would not be posted abroad. In 1906 their daughter, May, was born, followed by Rupert in 1907 and Maurice in 1910. Like her cousins, Alix and Irene of Hesse and Ena of Battenberg, Princess Alice was a carrier of haemophilia and she passed the disease to both sons. Prince Maurice died six months after his birth, but Prince Rupert, despite his handicap, grew to be a charming and adventurous young man. He died in 1928, aged twenty-one, following a car accident in France. Princess May married Sir Henry Abel Smith in 1931, and they had three children.

Alice and Alge endured a prolonged separation during the First World War, when he was attached to the Belgian Army. During the four years of the war they spent little more than six weeks together. In 1917, when George V decreed that the royal family should abandon their German titles, Prince Alexander was created Earl of Athlone. Princess May became Lady May Cambridge, and Prince Rupert was given the title Viscount Trematon. Princess Alice was a British princess in her own right, and so she retained her title and royal rank. Alge was furious with these changes, regarding them as undignified and unnecessary.

After the war, Alge, now Earl of Athlone whether he liked it or not, became Chancellor of the universities of London, Oxford and Cambridge, and in 1924 he was appointed Governor-General of South Africa in succession to Alice's cousin, Arthur of Connaught. He was a

(Left) *Princess Alice and the Earl of Athlone in 1933, on their departure from Waterloo for a return visit to South Africa.* (Below) *The Princess and her husband photographed on a more formal occasion in 1935.*

popular and tactful Governor-General, much liked by all sections of the population, and he and Alice returned there regularly after his term of office came to an end in 1930. Further foreign visits followed, to the Bahamas, India and Arabia, until Alge became Governor-General of Canada from 1940 to 1945.

After Alge's death in 1957, Princess Alice continued to lead a full and active life. She spent each winter in the Caribbean where, in 1950, she had become Chancellor of the University of the West Indies. In 1966 she published her memoirs, *For My Grandchildren*.

Throughout her long and active life, Princess Alice retained a sparkling personality and a talent for conversation. Her fascinating recollections of Queen Victoria and events from her childhood and youth entertained millions during television interviews towards the end of her life, and she was the only person present at the Queen's Silver Jubilee Service in 1977 who could remember Queen Victoria's Golden Jubilee celebrations, ninety years before. When Princess Alice died on 3 January 1981, at the age of ninety-seven years and 313 days, she had become the longest-living member of the British royal family and the last survivor of Queen Victoria's forty grandchildren.

(Above) *Prince Charles Edward aged fifteen, at the time of his move to Germany.* (Below) *The Prince with his wife, Princess Victoria Adelheid of Schleswig-Holstein-Sonderburg-Glücksburg, soon after his accession to the Dukedom of Saxe-Coburg and Gotha.*

Charles Edward, Duke of Saxe-Coburg and Gotha 1884–1954

Prince Leopold had always been fascinated by Bonnie Prince Charlie and the Stuarts, and it was he who decided that, if his second child were a boy, he should be called Charles Edward in honour of the 'Young Pretender'. Sadly, Leopold did not live to see the birth of his only son, for he died four months before Charles Edward's birth in July 1884. When he was fourteen years old, his cousin, Alfred of Edinburgh, died, leaving the Duke of Saxe-Coburg and Gotha without an heir. The succession was then rejected by the Duke of Connaught and his son before passing to the reluctant and bewildered Charlie. He was told that he would have to leave Eton immediately and go and live in Germany, where he would be educated for his future position as a reigning Duke.

The entire family were distressed by this upheaval. Charlie's mother hated the thought of parting with her son and seeing him changed from an English prince into a German one. But, upsetting though it was, Charlie had no choice but to move to Germany, accompanied by his mother and sister.

In 1903, the Duchess of Albany and Princess Alice returned to England, leaving Charlie on his own, and in 1905, when he turned twenty-one, he assumed full control of his small Duchy. Three months later he married Princess Victoria Adelheid of Schleswig-Holstein-Sonderburg-Glücksburg, a niece of the Empress Auguste Viktoria of Germany. Their marriage was extremely happy and they had five children, including Princess Sibylla, who married the eldest son of the Crown Prince of Sweden and became the mother of the present King Carl Gustaf.

By the time of the First World War, Charlie had risen to become a General in the Prussian Guards, and the outbreak of hostilities placed him in an agonising position. He decided that he could not fight against the country of his birth and asked to be sent to the Russian Front instead. The war finally shattered Charlie's spirit. He was denounced in Germany for being English and in England for being German, and, in 1919, all his British titles were struck from the Roll of Peers by Order in Council.

When he was reunited with his mother and sister in 1921, Charlie was no longer reigning Duke of Saxe-Coburg, but he now identified himself completely with his country of adoption. During the 1930s he became increasingly active in reactionary and militarist organisations, and in 1935 he joined the Nazi Party.

In the years preceding the Second World War, Charlie became obsessed with the idea of an Anglo-German alliance, believing himself to be ideally qualified to bring this about. With the encouragement of Hitler, he made several visits to London for talks with prominent personalities, but the outbreak of war brought these discussions to an end.

At the end of the war, Coburg came under United States control. Charlie and his wife were left alone by General Patton, but his less sympathetic successor sent the Duke to a prisoner-of-war camp. By now crippled with arthritis, Charlie was released in 1946, and he and Victoria Adelheid settled in a small cottage attached to the stables of Schloss Callenburg. It was there, in 1948, that his sister Alice and the Earl of Athlone discovered them living in appalling conditions. The Athlones managed to persuade the authorities to allow Charlie and his wife better housing, and he was eventually permitted to move into a wing of one of his own properties. In 1949, Charlie was found guilty by a war crimes tribunal of being a member of the Nazi Party and various other minor wartime offences, and fined. Five years later he died, aged sixty-nine, broken in health and in spirit.

Following his military training in Potsdam, Prince Charles Edward joined the First Regiment of Guards, and the transformation of the Eton schoolboy into a Prussian soldier was complete.

The Children of Beatrice and Henry

Alexander
Marquess of Carisbrooke
1886–1960

Victoria Eugenie
Queen of Spain
1887–1969

Leopold
Lord Leopold Mountbatten
1889–1922

Maurice
Prince of Battenberg
1891–1914

Beatrice & Henry of Battenberg

Princess Beatrice was four years old when her father died and, in the melancholy atmosphere that prevailed after Prince Albert's death, she lost all charm and spontaneity and became instead an awkward, shy and withdrawn little girl. As the youngest of Victoria's daughters, her childhood was solitary and isolated. The Queen was determined that Beatrice should never leave her but 'be the prop, comfort and companion of her widowed mother to old age,' and so, despite her intelligence and artistic gifts, she grew up to be dull and shy with others. Her diffidence and lack of conventional beauty did not inhibit rumours of marriage, but the Queen would not consider any match for her youngest child.

In 1884, Beatrice attended the wedding of her niece, Victoria of Hesse, to Prince Louis of Battenberg and there fell in love with the bridegroom's brother, Henry. When Beatrice informed her mother of her intention to marry Prince Henry, the Queen's response was angry and immediate. Not only did she refuse to allow the marriage but she also declined to speak to her daughter for seven months. All through the summer of 1884, communication between the Queen and Princess Beatrice was limited to notes pushed across the breakfast table. The Queen relented at last, following persuasion from other members of her family, and gave her permission on condition that Beatrice and Henry agree to live with her after their marriage. Prince Henry was a devoted husband and father, but he found life dull with his mother-in-law and insisted on joining the British Expeditionary Force to Ashanti in 1895, where he contracted malaria and died in January 1896.

After Queen Victoria's death five years later, Beatrice spent much of her time transcribing her mother's diaries. The Queen had instructed her to modify or destroy any unsuitable passages and so, over the next forty years, the Princess censored her mother's journals, burning the original manuscript in the process. Princess Beatrice died in October 1944.

Alexander, Marquess of Carisbrooke
1886–1960

Prince Alexander of Battenberg at the time of the First World War.

The birth of Prince Alexander in 1886 gave Queen Victoria a new lease of life. For the first time in many years, there was a baby living in her home, and she took great delight in the knowledge that Drino, as he was called, was sleeping in the nursery right above her private sitting-room.

The early years of Drino's childhood were spent happily at Windsor and the Queen's other homes. The presence of Drino and, later, his sister and brothers gave the old Queen great pleasure, and these grandchildren soon became her favourites. She enjoyed spoiling them – on Drino's eleventh birthday she gave him a party that included a film show and performing dogs – and when Drino was sent away to school at Wellington College he missed his grandmother far more than he did his mother.

Drino's schooldays at Wellington were not the happiest of his life. The boys there considered him to be conceited and precious, while he in his turn regarded them as 'bloodthirsty hooligans'. Because he was unaccustomed to handling cash, Drino had great difficulty managing his finances and on one occasion he was forced to ask his grandmother for money. She wrote back to say that he must learn to live within his allowance. A few days later, Drino wrote to the Queen again to tell her that he was no longer in difficulties because he had sold her letter to another boy.

From Wellington, Drino went into the Royal Navy, from 1902 until 1908, and then he was commissioned in the Grenadier Guards during the First World War. Although Drino was mentioned in despatches, his fellow Grenadier, the Prince of Wales, was not at all impressed. 'The completest dud I always think,' wrote the future Edward VIII.

When his cousin, George V, abolished the royal family's German titles in 1917, Drino reluctantly lost his princely title and style of 'Highness' and became instead the Marquess of Carisbrooke. In the same year he married Lady Irene Denison, only daughter of the Earl of

(Above left) *Princess Beatrice and Prince Henry of Battenberg with the infant Prince Alexander in January 1887.*
(Above right) *Prince Alexander* (centre) *with Prince Leopold and Princess Ena.*

Londesborough. A few months later the Prince of Wales had a further acerbic comment to make about his relative. 'I hear that Irene Carisbrooke has signs of a baby and that Drino has retired to bed for a month's rest cure!' The baby was to be Drino's only child, Lady Iris Mountbatten. She married three times and led an eventful life in the United States and Canada that resulted in her estrangement from her relations in England.

After the war, Drino became the first member of the royal family to go into business. He trained as a junior clerk with the banking house of Lazard Brothers, and was later offered the directorship of several important companies; he also became Senior Steward of the Greyhound Racing Club. During the Second World War he served in the Royal Air Force as a non-flying Pilot Officer.

Drino was an entertaining and popular figure, who enjoyed music and gossip. One of his guests once described him as 'immaculately dressed in a well-pressed check suit, padded shoulders, and jangling gold bracelets and rings. He reminded me of an old spruce hen, cackling and scratching the dust in a chicken-run.' He died in 1960.

Victoria Eugenie, Queen of Spain
1887–1969

Princess Ena and King Alfonso at the time of their engagement in 1905. The King's mother, the formidable Dowager Queen Maria Cristina, would have preferred her son to have married one of his Austrian cousins.

Princess Beatrice's only daughter came into the world at Balmoral Castle, the first royal child to be born in Scotland since 1600. She was christened Victoria Eugenie Julia Ena, the first and third names being chosen to please her two grandmothers, and the second in honour of her godmother, the Empress Eugénie of France, who had become a close friend of Queen Victoria during her exile in England. Ena, an old Gaelic name, was chosen to mark the child's Scottish birth, and it was by this that the young princess was usually known.

The childhood of Princess Ena was dominated by Queen Victoria. The princess and her brothers spent a good part of each day with the Queen and their relationship became particularly close. 'I love these darling children, almost as much as their own parents,' the Queen once said, and her affection was returned by these lively and attractive grandchildren. Ena was a healthy, outspoken child who shared the outdoor interests of her brothers, but her lively appearance concealed a sensitive nature. 'I fear she will never find life easy,' her aunt, the Empress Friedrich, noted sadly.

Princess Ena grew to be a beautiful and dignified young woman, and she soon began to attract the attention of foreign princes. When she was seventeen, Grand Duke Boris of Russia fell in love with her and proposed marriage but Ena declined. Then, in 1905, the young King Alfonso XIII of Spain came to England on a state visit, and Ena had no doubt at all where her future lay. She and Alfonso fell in love and when their marriage was proposed she accepted.

Alfonso, who had been born King of Spain, was nineteen years old when he visited England, and in urgent need of a wife, not solely for dynastic reasons. The King had inherited the promiscuous nature of his forebears and it was hoped that a wife might divert his roving eye, for a while. Despite his amorous inclinations, Alfonso was hardly an enticing suitor, with his spindly physique, pale face and long Hapsburg nose and jaw, but he had enormous charm, and women were reputed to find his large, dark eyes irresistible.

The choice of Ena as Queen of Spain did not meet with universal approval. Although she immediately converted to Roman Catholicism and renounced her rights to the British throne, Ena was regarded by many at the stiff and hidebound Spanish court as a Protestant heretic.

The wedding took place in Madrid on 31 May, 1906, and Ena then became Queen Victoria Eugenia of Spain. The day was marked by a tragedy that almost ended Ena's reign before it had begun, and seemed a dark omen for the years ahead. As the wedding procession wound its spectacular way through the crowded streets from the church to the Royal Palace, a young man called Mateo Morral flung a bouquet towards the coach carrying the King and his bride. Fortunately the bouquet did not land in the coach but a little ahead of it, for concealed among the flowers was a bomb. Over one hundred people were injured by the explosion, and twenty-four died, including a guardsman riding beside the coach whose blood splashed over Ena's wedding dress. Neither she nor Alfonso was injured. The Spanish were mystified by Ena's reaction to the tragedy. As a British princess brought up to maintain her dignity and decorum at all costs, she refused to show any panic or distress at what had happened, but onlookers mistook her calmness for coldness and lack of concern.

In the early years of her marriage, Ena had to contend with the suspicious and hostile attitude of the court as well as the people. After the comparative simplicity of life at Windsor and Osborne, she found the rigid ceremonial of the Spanish court needlessly restrictive, and she was taken aback by the harsh contrasts in Spanish landscape and society. She was especially appalled by the sickening violence of the bullfight, until her brother, Alexander, advised her to adjust the focus of her field-glasses so that she needn't see the slaughter at all.

Ena's position might have been easier had she been able to provide Alfonso with healthy heirs, but only one of their four sons was to lead a completely healthy life. Their first son, Alfonso, was born in 1907, and soon after the birth it was discovered that the prince was haemophiliac. King Alfonso was devastated by the news, and blamed Ena, her mother and even Queen Victoria for concealing the possibility that his wife might be a carrier of the disease. But Ena and many others had warned him before the marriage that the possibility existed; it was by then no secret that the female descendants of Victoria were carriers of what was called 'the English disease'. Ena was to have six more children in swift succession. Of these, the second son, Jaime, became a deaf mute following an operation for double mastoiditis when he was

Princess Ena with her brothers, Prince Leopold (left) *and Prince Alexander. They spent their childhood with Queen Victoria and became her favourite grandchildren.*

(Left) *Ena and Alfonso with their first child, Alfonso, Prince of the Asturias.* (Centre) *Ena with Alfonso.* (Right) *Ena with her three eldest children, Alfonso, Beatriz and Jaime. Alfonso was a haemophiliac and Jaime became a deaf mute when he was three, following an unsuccessful operation.*

three, and the youngest, Gonzalo, also suffered from haemophilia. Only Juan, born in 1913, was completely healthy. He became head of the Royal House on the death of King Alfonso, and is the father of the present King Juan Carlos I. A fourth son was stillborn in 1910. Ena's two daughters, Beatriz and Maria Cristina, both married Italian aristocrats.

Unlike her cousin Alix, whose marriage was strengthened even further by the discovery of her son's haemophilia, Ena found that her relationship with Alfonso was destroyed by their shared misfortune. He turned away from her and found consolation instead with a succession of mistresses.

During the 1920s the growing republican movement in Spain was fuelled by the dictatorship of Miguel Primo de Rivera. When the army withdrew its support from him in 1930 he went into exile, and after the municipal elections in the following year recorded an overwhelming majority in favour of republican government, Alfonso, too, left Spain for good. Ena soon followed him, with their children.

Ena and Alfonso spent the first months of their exile in Paris but it was not long before they parted. Their separation was unpleasant and explosive, with Alfonso accusing Ena of having love affairs with both the Duke *and* Duchess of Lucera, and they were never reconciled. Ena spent the next ten years in England, France and Italy, and after the Second World War she settled permanently in Lausanne. Alfonso never gave up hope of returning to Spain as King, and General Franco's victory in the Spanish Civil War seemed at first to herald a restoration of the monarchy. But Franco told Alfonso that the time was not yet right and, in any case, when a King *did* return to Spain he would make sure that it was not him. Ena's eldest and youngest sons, Alfonso and Gonzalo, were killed in car accidents in 1938 and 1934, and then the King himself died in Rome in 1941, aged fifty-four.

Ena survived Alfonso by nearly thirty years. In 1968, the year before her death, she returned at last to Spain, where she attended the christening of her great-grandson, Felipe, and was welcomed by enthusiastic crowds. Sadly, she did not live to see the monarchy restored and the accession to the throne of her grandson, Juan Carlos, seven years later.

(Left) *Queen Ena had a lifelong love of horses. During her early years in Spain, the sufferings of horses in the bullring caused her great distress.* (Right) *The exiled Queen Ena in 1934. In her later years, she became known as the most elegant Queen in Europe.*

Lord Leopold Mountbatten

1889–1922

Both Leopold and his younger brother, Maurice, inherited haemophilia from their mother, and the disease was to have tragic consequences for both of them. As a child, Leopold dreamed of becoming a soldier but his delicate health made him unfit for military service and, after leaving school at Wellington, he went to Magdalene College, Cambridge. He also travelled widely in Canada, Australia, India and Japan.

In 1914, Prince Leopold would not rest until he was allowed to join the Forces and, despite constant ill-health, he enlisted in the King's Royal Rifles and served in France, eventually reaching the rank of Major. In 1917, in common with his surviving brother, he relinquished his royal style and title and became Lord Leopold Mountbatten.

Leopold was the most intellectual of Princess Beatrice's children, and he was also a talented musician. Queen Victoria always enjoyed hearing him play the violin, usually accompanied by his mother or a lady-in-waiting, and his playing soothed the Queen during her final hours.

In 1922, Leopold fell ill and underwent emergency surgery at Kensington Palace. Although at first he appeared to make a normal recovery, he suffered a relapse and died, aged thirty-three.

(Above) *Prince Leopold as a young man and* (below) *with his mother, Princess Beatrice, and his brothers, Maurice* (left) *and Alexander* (seated) *at the Coronation of King George V in 1911.*

Prince Maurice of Battenberg
1891–1914

The last of Queen Victoria's grandchildren was also the second to be born in Scotland, and great celebrations marked the arrival of Prince Maurice at Balmoral in 1891. He was christened Maurice Victor Donald, the last name in tribute to the country of his birth.

Maurice was the liveliest of Princess Beatrice's sons, and early on he decided on a career in the Army, despite the fact that he, like his brother Leopold, suffered from haemophilia. He was deeply upset by the death of his cousin, Prince Christian Victor, in the Boer War and it was then, at the age of nine, that he told Christian Victor's sister, Helena Victoria, that he had decided to join his cousin's regiment, the 60th King's Royal Rifles, when he was old enough. Maurice did indeed join this regiment in 1911 when he left Sandhurst, but he also developed an interest in aviation and made several solo flights. He had hoped to become a pilot in the Royal Flying Corps but, when the First World War broke out, he went with his regiment to France and fought in the front line from the very first engagement. On 27 October, 1914, less than three months after the beginning of hostilities, the Prince was leading his company in an attack near Mons when he was struck by a piece of shrapnel and died almost immediately.

Princess Beatrice was told that an exception would be made in this case and Prince Maurice's body returned to England for burial, but the Princess refused to accept such preferential treatment and asked that her son be buried in Belgium among his fallen comrades.

(Above) *Prince Maurice with a feline friend and* (below) *with his brother, Leopold* (left) *at Nice in 1895* (detail).

Select Bibliography

Of the many books that have been published about Queen Victoria and her descendants, the following have proved particularly helpful during the writing of this one.

Alice, Princess, Countess of Athlone, *For My Grandchildren*, Evans, 1966.

Almedingen, E.M., *An Unbroken Unity: A Memoir of Grand-Duchess Serge of Russia 1864–1918*, The Bodley Head, 1964.

Aronson, Theo, *Grandmama of Europe: The Crowned Descendants of Queen Victoria*, Cassell, 1973.

— *Princess Alice Countess of Athlone*, Cassell, 1981.

Battiscombe, Georgina *Queen Alexandra*, Constable, 1969.

Bennett, Daphne, *Vicky: Princess Royal of England and German Empress*, Collins, 1971.

Buchanan, Meriel, *Queen Victoria's Relations*, Cassell, 1954.

Cookridge, E.H., *From Battenberg to Mountbatten*, Arthur Barker, 1966.

Cyril, Grand Duke of Russia, *My Life in Russia's Service – Then and Now*, Selwyn and Blount, 1939.

Daisy, Princess of Pless, *Daisy Princess of Pless By Herself*, John Murray, 1928.

— *From My Private Diary*, John Murray, 1931.

Diesbach, Ghislain de, *Secrets of the Gotha*, Chapman and Hall, 1967.

Duff, David, *Hessian Tapestry*, Frederick Muller, 1967.

— *The Shy Princess: The Life of Her Royal Highness Princess Beatrice*, Evans, 1958.

Eilers, Marlene A., *Queen Victoria's Descendants*, Atlantic International, 1987.

Elsberry, Terence, *Marie of Romania*, Cassell, 1973.

Hough, Richard, *Louis and Victoria: The First Mountbattens*, Hutchinson, 1974.

Kidd, Charles and Montague-Smith, Patrick, *Debrett's Book of Royal Children*, Debrett's Peerage, 1982.

Lees-Milne, James, *The Enigmatic Edwardian: The Life of Reginald, 2nd Viscount Esher*, Sidgwick and Jackson, 1986.

Leslie, Anita, *Edwardians in Love*, Hutchinson, 1972.

Longford, Elizabeth, *Victoria R.I.*, Weidenfeld and Nicolson, 1964.

Lynx, J.J., *The Great Hohenzollern Scandal: A Biography of Alexander Zubkov*, Oldbourne, 1965.

Magnus, Philip, *King Edward the Seventh*, John Murray, 1964.

Mallet, Marie, *Life with Queen Victoria: Marie Mallet's Letters from Court 1887–1901*, John Murray, 1968.

Marie, Queen of Roumania, *The Story of My Life*, 3 vols., Cassell, 1934–5.

Marie Louise, Princess, *My Memories of Six Reigns*, Evans, 1956.

Massie, Robert K., *Nicholas and Alexandra*, Victor Gollancz, 1968.

Montgomery-Massingberd, Hugh (editor), *Burke's Royal Families of the World. Vol. I. Europe and Latin America*, Burke's Peerage, 1977.

Nicholas, Prince of Greece, *My Fifty Years*, Hutchinson, 1926.

Noel, Gerard, *Ena: Spain's English Queen*, Constable, 1984.

— *Princess Alice: Queen Victoria's Forgotten Daughter*, Constable, 1974.

Pakula, Hannah, *The Last Romantic: A Biography of Queen Marie of Roumania*, Weidenfeld and Nicolson, 1985.

Pope-Hennessy, James, *Queen Mary 1867–1953*, George Allen and Unwin, 1959.

Rose, Kenneth, *King George V*, Weidenfeld and Nicolson, 1983.

— *Kings, Queens and Courtiers*, Weidenfeld and Nicolson, 1985.

Van Der Kiste, John and Jordaan, Bee, *Dearest Affie: Alfred, Duke of Edinburgh, Queen Victoria's Second Son 1844–1900*, Alan Sutton, 1984.

Victoria, German Empress, *The Empress Frederick Writes to Sophie*, edited by Arthur Gould Lee. Faber and Faber, 1955.

Victoria, Princess of Prussia, *My Memoirs*, Eveleigh Nash and Grayson, 1929.

Victoria, Queen of Great Britain, *Advice to a Grand-daughter: Letters from Queen Victoria to Princess Victoria of Hesse*, edited by Richard Hough. Heinemann, 1975.

— *Dearest Child: Letters between Queen Victoria and the Princess Royal 1858–1861*, edited by Roger Fulford. Evans, 1965.

— *Dearest Mama: Letters between Queen Victoria and the Crown Princess of Prussia 1861–1864*, edited by Roger Fulford. Evans, 1968.

— *Your Dear Letter: Private Correspondence of Queen Victoria and the Crown Princess of Prussia 1865–1871*, edited by Roger Fulford. Evans, 1971.

— *Darling Child: Private Correspondence of Queen Victoria and the Crown Princess of Prussia 1871–1878*, edited by Roger Fulford. Evans, 1976.

— *Beloved Mama: Private Correspondence of Queen Victoria and the German Crown Princess 1878–1885*, edited by Roger Fulford. Evans, 1981.

— *Beloved and Darling Child: Last Letters between Queen Victoria and Her Eldest Daughter 1886–1901*, edited by Agatha Ramm. Alan Sutton, 1990.

Vorres, Ian, *The Last Grand-Duchess: Her Imperial Highness Grand-Duchess Olga Alexandrovna 1882–1960*, Hutchinson, 1960.

Acknowledgements

The publishers and the author would like to thank the following for their kind permission to reproduce the photographs in this book.

The Royal Archives, Windsor Castle. Copyright reserved. Reproduced by gracious permission of H.M. the Queen.
Cover (detail), p. 12, 17, 19, 20, 21 (detail), 22, 26, 30, 31, 37 (top right), 57, 58 (bottom), 59 (bottom), 60, 61, 63, 66, 68, 75, 78, 79, 86 (top), 87, 88, 90 (bottom), 94, 95, 96, 97, 99, 101, 107 (top), 116 (top), 121 (left), 126 (bottom) detail, 127 (bottom).

The Trustees of the Broadlands Archive Trust
p. 59 (top), 62 (bottom left), 64, 67, 86 (bottom).

The Hulton Picture Company
p. 13, 14 (and cover), 15, 16, 18, 23, 24, 25, 34, 35, 36, 37, 39, 40, 41, 42, 43, 44, 45, 46, 48, 50, 51, 52, 58 (top), 62, 65, 70 (top right), 71, 72, 73, 74, 80 (bottom left), 81, 82 (top), 83 (bottom), 84, 85, 91 (top), 104 (bottom), 106 (bottom), 109, 112, 115, 117, 121 (right), 123, 124 (middle and right), 125 (and cover), 127 (bottom), back cover.

Author's private collection
Cover, p. 20 (bottom), 27, 28, 29, 43 (top), 44 (bottom), 45 (bottom right), 47, 52 (bottom left), 69, 70 (top left), 80 (bottom left), 81, 82 (left), 83 (top right), 89, 90 (top), 91 (bottom), 98, 100, 105, 106 (top), 107 (bottom), 108 (and cover), 113, 114, 116 (bottom) 120, 122, 124 (left), 126 (top), 127 (top and cover).